Overcoming Common Problems

Helping Children Get the Most from School

Sarah Lawson

First published in Great Britain in 2002 by
Sheldon Press
1 Marylebone Road
London NW1 4DU

British Library Cataloguing-in-Publication Data

A catalogue record for this book is available from the British
Library

ISBN 0-85969-864-5 ✔

Typeset by Deltatype Limited, Birkenhead, Merseyside
Printed in Great Britain by Biddles Ltd
www.biddles.co.uk

Overcoming Common Problems Series

Coping with Stammering
Trudy Stewart and Jackie Turnbull

Coping with Stomach Ulcers
Dr Tom Smith

Coping with Strokes
Dr Tom Smith

Coping with Thrush
Caroline Clayton

Coping with Thyroid Problems
Dr Joan Gomez

Curing Arthritis – The Drug-Free Way
Margaret Hills

**Curing Arthritis – More ways to a
drug-free life**
Margaret Hills

Curing Arthritis Diet Book
Margaret Hills

Curing Arthritis Exercise Book
Margaret Hills and Janet Horwood

Cystic Fibrosis – A Family Affair
Jane Chumbley

Depression
Dr Paul Hauck

Depression at Work
Vicky Maud

**Everything Parents Should Know
About Drugs**
Sarah Lawson

Fertility
Julie Reid

Feverfew
Dr Stewart Johnson

Gambling – A Family Affair
Angela Willans

Garlic
Karen Evennett

Getting a Good Night's Sleep
Fiona Johnston

The Good Stress Guide
Mary Hartley

Heart Attacks – Prevent and Survive
Dr Tom Smith

**Helping Children Cope with Attention
Deficit Disorder**
Dr Patricia Gilbert

Helping Children Cope with Bullying
Sarah Lawson

Helping Children Cope with Divorce
Rosemary Wells

Helping Children Cope with Grief
Rosemary Wells

Helping Children Cope with Stammering
Jackie Turnbull and Trudy Stewart

Hold Your Head Up High
Dr Paul Hauck

How to Accept Yourself
Dr Windy Dryden

How to Be Your Own Best Friend
Dr Paul Hauck

How to Cope when the Going Gets Tough
Dr Windy Dryden and Jack Gordon

How to Cope with Anaemia
Dr Joan Gomez

How to Cope with Bulimia
Dr Joan Gomez

How to Cope with Difficult Parents
Dr Windy Dryden and Jack Gordon

How to Cope with Difficult People
Alan Houel with Christian Godefroy

**How to Cope with People who Drive
You Crazy**
Dr Paul Hauck

How to Cope with Stress
Dr Peter Tyrer

How to Enjoy Your Retirement
Vicky Maud

How to Get Where You Want to Be
Christian Godefroy

How to Improve Your Confidence
Dr Kenneth Hambly

How to Interview and Be Interviewed
Michele Brown and Gyles Brandreth

How to Keep Your Cholesterol in Check
Dr Robert Povey

How to Lose Weight Without Dieting
Mark Barker

How to Love and Be Loved
Dr Paul Hauck

How to Pass Your Driving Test
Donald Ridland

How to Raise Confident Children
Carole Baldock

How to Stand up for Yourself
Dr Paul Hauck

**How to Start a Conversation and Make
Friends**
Don Gabor

Overcoming Common Problems Series

How to Stick to a Diet
Deborah Steinberg and Dr Windy Dryden

How to Stop Worrying
Dr Frank Tallis

The How to Study Book
Alan Brown

How to Succeed as a Single Parent
Carole Baldock

How to Untangle Your Emotional Knots
Dr Windy Dryden and Jack Gordon

How to Write a Successful CV
Joanna Gutmann

Hysterectomy
Suzie Hayman

The Irritable Bowel Diet Book
Rosemary Nicol

The Irritable Bowel Stress Book
Rosemary Nicol

Is HRT Right for You?
Dr Anne MacGregor

Jealousy
Dr Paul Hauck

Living with Asthma
Dr Robert Youngson

Living with Crohn's Disease
Dr Joan Gomez

Living with Diabetes
Dr Joan Gomez

Living with Fibromyalgia
Christine Craggs-Hinton

Living with Grief
Dr Tony Lake

Living with High Blood Pressure
Dr Tom Smith

Living with Nut Allergies
Karen Evennett

Living with Osteoporosis
Dr Joan Gomez

Living with a Stoma
Dr Craig White

Making Friends with Your Stepchildren
Rosemary Wells

Motor Neurone Disease – A Family Affair
Dr David Oliver

Overcoming Anger
Dr Windy Dryden

Overcoming Anxiety
Dr Windy Dryden

Overcoming Guilt
Dr Windy Dryden

Overcoming Jealousy
Dr Windy Dryden

Overcoming Procrastination
Dr Windy Dryden

Overcoming Shame
Dr Windy Dryden

Overcoming Your Addictions
Dr Windy Dryden and
Dr Walter Matweychuk

The Parkinson's Disease Handbook
Dr Richard Godwin-Austen

The PMS Diet Book
Karen Evennett

A Positive Thought for Every Day
Dr Windy Dryden

Rheumatoid Arthritis
Mary-Claire Mason and Dr Elaine Smith

Second Time Around
Anne Lovell

Serious Mental Illness – A Family Affair
Gwen Howe

Shift Your Thinking, Change Your Life
Mo Shapiro

The Stress Workbook
Joanna Gutmann

The Subfertility Handbook
Virginia Ironside and Sarah Biggs

Successful Au Pairs
Hilli Matthews

Talking with Confidence
Don Gabor

Ten Steps to Positive Living
Dr Windy Dryden

Think Your Way to Happiness
Dr Windy Dryden and Jack Gordon

The Travellers' Good Health Guide
Ted Lankester

Understanding Obsessions and Compulsions
Dr Frank Tallis

Understanding Sex and Relationships
Rosemary Stones

Understanding Your Personality
Patricia Hedges

Work–Life Balance
Gordon and Ronni Lamont

Sarah Lawson was born in London, and brought up in rural Oxfordshire. She spent five years as a postal counsellor and leaflet writer for the *Woman's Own* magazine problem page, and now works as a freelance journalist. She has written widely on family issues, including two earlier books for Sheldon Press, *Helping Children Cope with Bullying* and *Everything Parents Should Know About Drugs*. She lives in Devon and has four children.

Overcoming Common Problems Series

For a full list of titles please contact
Sheldon Press, Marylebone Road, London NW1 4DU

Antioxidants
Dr Robert Youngson

The Assertiveness Workbook
Joanna Gutmann

Beating the Comfort Trap
Dr Windy Dryden and Jack Gordon

Body Language
Allan Pease

Body Language in Relationships
David Cohen

Calm Down
Dr Paul Hauck

Cancer – A Family Affair
Neville Shone

The Cancer Guide for Men
Helen Beare and Neil Priddy

The Candida Diet Book
Karen Brody

Caring for Your Elderly Parent
Julia Burton-Jones

Cider Vinegar
Margaret Hills

Comfort for Depression
Janet Horwood

Considering Adoption?
Sarah Biggs

Coping Successfully with Hay Fever
Dr Robert Youngson

Coping Successfully with Pain
Neville Shone

Coping Successfully with Panic Attacks
Shirley Trickett

Coping Successfully with PMS
Karen Evennett

Coping Successfully with Prostate Problems
Rosy Reynolds

Coping Successfully with RSI
Maggie Black and Penny Gray

Coping Successfully with Your Hiatus Hernia
Dr Tom Smith

Coping Successfully with Your Irritable Bladder
Dr Jennifer Hunt

Coping Successfully with Your Irritable Bowel
Rosemary Nicol

Coping When Your Child Has Special Needs
Suzanne Askham

Coping with Anxiety and Depression
Shirley Trickett

Coping with Blushing
Dr Robert Edelmann

Coping with Bronchitis and Emphysema
Dr Tom Smith

Coping with Candida
Shirley Trickett

Coping with Chronic Fatigue
Trudie Chalder

Coping with Coeliac Disease
Karen Brody

Coping with Cystitis
Caroline Clayton

Coping with Depression and Elation
Dr Patrick McKeon

Coping with Eczema
Dr Robert Youngson

Coping with Endometriosis
Jo Mears

Coping with Epilepsy
Fiona Marshall and
Dr Pamela Crawford

Coping with Fibroids
Mary-Claire Mason

Coping with Gallstones
Dr Joan Gomez

Coping with Headaches and Migraine
Shirley Trickett

Coping with a Hernia
Dr David Delvin

Coping with Long-Term Illness
Barbara Baker

Coping with the Menopause
Janet Horwood

Coping with Psoriasis
Professor Ronald Marks

Coping with Rheumatism and Arthritis
Dr Robert Youngson

To Callum

Contents

Acknowledgements   x

Introduction   xi

 1 Choosing a School or Pre-school Group   1
 2 Communicating with the School   21
 3 Expectations and Motivation   37
 4 Building Confidence   47
 5 Health, Happiness and the Ability to Learn   55
 6 Practical Ways to Help   67
 7 Homework   83
 8 When Things Go Wrong   89
 9 The Gifted Child and the Underachiever   109
10 Home Education – An Alternative?   117
11 Special Needs   123

Useful Addresses   133
Further Reading   143
Index   145

Acknowledgements

So many people contributed to this book that there isn't room to name them all. I would especially like to thank all the teachers, parents and children who responded to my requests for help, both in person and over the Internet – many went to enormous trouble to send me detailed accounts of their experiences, or endured lengthy interviews with remarkable cheerfulness, and although not all the stories they told me have made it into the finished book, they all contributed immeasurably to my understanding of the relationship between home and school, and many other issues surrounding education. Toni Carter, David Andrews and Bob Brewer, whose collective years 'on active service' in education must total well over half a century, were particularly inspirational.

On the more practical side, I have to thank Angela Willans and Bob Stephenson for the use of their proofreading skills, and my own four children, whose combined experience (so far) of nine schools and five pre-school groups have given me an extended insight into the world of school, and taught me what questions to ask.

Introduction

In 1999, 71 per cent of 11-year-olds in English state schools reached the expected standard for their age in literacy, and 69 per cent in numeracy. These figures show a steady improvement in the achievements of schoolchildren, but there is no room for complacency. Many children – nobody knows how many, since national learning targets provide only a very rough guide to attainment – are failing to reach their full potential.

Why do some children sail through school with flying colours, while others struggle? There are many reasons, but one factor has been pinpointed again and again both by scientific research and by the observations of teachers – parental involvement. Children whose parents take an active interest in school and what happens there, and who help them, outside school, to expand on and add to what they learn there, simply do better than those whose parents don't. They are better motivated, more confident, and they learn more effectively.

We shouldn't be surprised by this. When parents and school work together, teachers can learn more from parents about the child's needs and abilities than they could hope to find out themselves in a crowded classroom. Problems can be caught early, before long-term damage is done, progress can be recognized and celebrated and activities at home can add a further dimension to the subjects the child studies at school. So why don't all parents get involved in their child's education?

In many cases, the answer is simply a lack of confidence. We often feel that teachers are the experts, and that we shouldn't try to intrude on their territory. Of course, teachers are highly trained professionals, with more knowledge and experience than most parents can hope to have of the way that children generally learn and behave. There is one area where your knowledge outstrips theirs, however – you are the world's foremost expert on your child. Good schools and good teachers know and value this.

In this book, I aim to give parents sound, practical advice that will enable them to approach their child's school with confidence. Starting with the choice of pre-school group or school, I explore and, I hope, clarify the way that school works, how parents can best communicate with teachers and how they can support their child's learning in very practical ways. I also look briefly at what parents can do to help children to grow up feeling good about themselves – confidence is mentioned again and again by teachers as an all-important factor in children's ability to learn.

Because things don't always go according to plan, I include chapters on what to do when things go wrong at school, and look at home education as a possible alternative to a school-based education. I also explore how parents can cope with their child's special educational needs, whether she is especially gifted or has a physical, developmental, emotional or behavioural problem that makes it more difficult to cope at school.

Most of the information in this book will apply throughout the UK, although there are minor differences in the way that schools are administered in some areas. Most will be equally applicable to both state and independent schools, although the administration arrangements will obviously be peculiar to each school in the independent sector, so complaints procedures will differ from those mentioned here.

It's always easier to get involved when you know what you're letting yourself in for, and I hope that this book will encourage parents to take an active interest in their child's education. I hope, too, that some will want to learn more about some of the subjects covered briefly here: how children learn, how families work, what makes a confident child. To this end, I have included a short list of further reading at the end of the book, as well as details of organizations that can provide information and courses on parenting.

1
Choosing a School or Pre-school Group

Unless you are going to educate your child at home (see Chapter 10), he must, by law, attend school from the start of the first term after his fifth birthday. From the start of the first term after his fourth birthday, he is entitled to three terms of free, part-time education, but there is no legal requirement for him to take this up. Parents are legally entitled to choose the school that their child will attend, but in practice the vast majority of children simply attend their local playgroup, then the designated state primary and secondary school for their catchment area. This has certain advantages:

- Children are educated within the community in which they are growing up, encouraging a feeling of belonging and involvement.
- The friends the child makes at school are likely to live nearby, and are therefore easily available for out-of-school socializing.
- After-school activities at the school will be more easily accessible.
- Transport to school for children living further than walking distance away will be arranged by the local authority, or can be shared with other local parents.

In many rural areas, secondary schools are so few and far between that attending one outside your own catchment area is practically impossible, although there may be a choice of primary school. In towns and cities, however, the situation can be quite different: within any given area there may be several primary and secondary schools to choose from, and the race to obtain a place for your child at what is seen as the 'best' school can become extremely competitive – and very stressful for all concerned.

Pre-school groups

Not all pre-school groups take part in the government's Early Education scheme, and only those that do can receive the grant that enables them to offer your child his free place. Many pre-school groups take children from 3, or even 2 years old. If you want to take advantage of your child's entitlement but are happy to pay for his attendance at a pre-school group before his fourth birthday, it makes sense to choose a group that is taking part in the scheme. That way, you avoid the disruption for your child of changing groups when he reaches his fourth birthday.

What's available?

Your local authority will be able to provide you with a list of pre-school groups and childminders in your area. All such groups must register with the local authority, and are subject to safety inspections and staff checks. All groups or individuals providing childcare, including childminders, are also inspected by OFSTED (in Scotland, Her Majesty's Inspectorate of Education).

Most pre-school groups fall into one of the following categories:

Playgroups (also known as playschools or pre-schools)

Age group:	3–5 years (sometimes from 2 years)
Early Education places:	Offered by some
Opening:	Variable, usually 3-hour sessions morning and/or afternoon
Minimum staffing:	1 adult to 8 children; at least half must be qualified

Playgroups have traditionally been parent-led, and less formal than nursery schools, but the gap has narrowed since the introduction of early learning targets. Children usually start with one or two sessions a week, adding more (if available) as they get older.

Day nurseries

Age group:	0–5 years
Early Education places:	Offered by some
Opening:	The whole working day
Minimum staffing:	1 adult to 8 children; at least half must be qualified

Day nurseries are primarily aimed at working parents, although most will also take children part-time.

Childminders

Age group:	Babies upwards
Early Education places:	Offered by some
Opening:	By arrangement with parents
Minimum staffing:	A childminder may look after 3 children at any one time, including her own

A childminder looks after children in her own home, and will often take care of school-age children after school hours, as well as pre-school children and babies.

Private nursery schools

Age group:	2–5 years
Early Education places:	Offered by some
Opening:	Half or full-day sessions, some open in school holidays
Minimum staffing:	1 adult to 13 children; at least half are qualified teachers

State nursery schools

Age group:	3 or 4 years–school start
Early Education places:	All places are free
Opening:	5 half-day sessions per week during term-time
Minimum staffing:	1 adult to 13 children, all qualified teachers or assistants

Nursery classes in state primary schools

Age group: 3–4 years–school start
Early Education places: All places are free
Opening: 5 half-day sessions per week during
                              term-time
Minimum staffing: 1 adult to 13 children, all qualified
                              teachers or assistants

Children will normally move into the reception or infant class in
the same school, although they can go to a different primary
school if parents wish.

Reception classes in state primary schools

Age group: 4–5 years
Early Education places: All places are free
Opening: 5 full-day sessions per week during
                              term-time (sometimes starting part-
                              time)
Minimum staffing: Usually 1 qualified teacher, often with
                              an assistant

Pre-school education can help your child to develop, through
play, the pre-reading, pre-mathematical, social and other skills
she will need to make the most of school. Some children will
make a start on reading and writing at pre-school, but many will
not be ready for formal learning at this early stage. For the child
who is ready to be away from her regular carer for a few hours,
playgroup or nursery can be a very positive experience, and most
teachers report that children who have attended a pre-school
group before starting school fit into the routines of a school day
more quickly and easily than those who haven't.

What to look for

As we have seen, pre-school groups are inspected in much the
same way as schools, and must show that they meet the standards
that the government has laid down for them. Nevertheless, there

4

is a good deal of variation between groups, and it is important that you choose a playgroup or nursery that will meet the individual needs of your child. A poorly run or ill-supervised group that fails to stimulate and interest the children in its care can make it hard for them to feel enthusiastic about school later on. Here are some points to bear in mind when you visit pre-school groups.

- *Supervision*: There are regulations governing the ratio of staff to children in pre-school groups, but these are of little use if three of the four adults present are chatting over a cup of coffee in the kitchen.
- *Involvement*: Playgroup and nursery staff are there for the benefit of the children. They should be spread about the room, getting involved with what the children are doing. If staff regularly congregate around one table, deep in conversation, they are not giving the children the attention they deserve.
- *Environment*: Surroundings should be kept clean and tidy, and equipment in good condition. Broken toys, puzzles with pieces missing, useless scissors and blunt pencils cause frustration, disappointment and discouragement, and should not be presented for children's use.
- *Discipline*: If staff often have to shout to keep order, to give lectures or tickings-off, or to use punishments like a 'naughty chair', they are probably making some basic mistakes in the running of the group. Each group should have a clearly defined policy for dealing with arguments and unruly behaviour, and should be able to tell you what that policy is.
- *Valuing individuals*: Like schools, many playgroups and nurseries do now have educational targets to meet, but there should still be plenty of room for each child to develop at his own pace, and to be valued for who he is, not what he can do. There is no hurry for children of this age to produce presentable 'work', paint recognizable pictures, write their names, colour inside the lines or any of the other things that parents and staff sometimes think are so important.

While pre-school groups can give your child a good start and help

5

to prepare him for school, this experience is not essential. Some children are just not ready to spend time outside the home without their principal carer before they reach school age (some, indeed, are still not ready when they do reach school age – see below) Some are ready at 4 but not at 3, some will need Mum to stay with them for many weeks before they feel confident enough to be left. Remember that your child need not go every day, and need not go at all if he really doesn't enjoy it. There are few experiences at playgroup or nursery that you cannot give your child at home if you are willing to put in a bit of time, effort and ingenuity.

The transition to school

Some primary schools operate an early admission policy, which means that many children now start primary school well before their fifth birthday. Most reception class teachers will agree that some children are simply not ready for school at this age, and problems can arise for both the pupil and her teacher when a child who is not sufficiently emotionally or developmentally mature is catapulted prematurely into the school environment.

James had been at the school's own nursery for the year before he started in the reception class. He had just about coped with that, although it took him ages to settle in and he was never very good at joining in organized activities. He is a very bright boy, although his coordination is quite poor for his age, and he bitterly resented being asked to stop an activity in which he was absorbed just because it was time to do something else.

He was two months away from his fifth birthday when he started school. I was a bit worried about how he'd cope, but all his friends were moving up and I just hoped that he'd be OK. He wasn't. He found the more structured day very hard to cope with, and simply refused to do what he was asked. The poor classroom assistant had to spend ages persuading him every time they wanted him to stop one activity and move on to

6

another, he hated assembly and found it terribly difficult to sit still while announcements were made, and his coordination was so poor that he found writing extremely difficult. He was really unhappy at school and cried every time I left him – his teacher had to hang on to him to prevent him from following me out of the building. It was absolutely awful.

He continued to be sullen, unhappy and disruptive at school for pretty much his whole first year, making very little progress with reading and writing, although he was always quick to answer questions and work things out verbally. Then, just around the time of his sixth birthday, there was an almost overnight transformation. He started bounding happily into school, his reading improved dramatically and he soon overtook the other children in his class, who had been far ahead of him for so long. His behaviour improved and he was obviously happy with his success and full of a new confidence. Everything seemed to fall into place, and his teacher and I both felt that he had simply not been ready for the whole school experience before, and now he was.

I wish that I had listened to my instincts and kept him in nursery until he was ready for school. He is doing really well now and, at 7, has been assessed as being unusually able, but his first year at school was not a positive experience for any of us.

We in the UK send our children off to school much earlier than many European countries, where 6 is a more usual starting age. Some children are just not ready for school at 5 or younger, and there is a danger that subjecting them to an experience that they are not really equipped to cope with will damage their confidence and put them off school indefinitely. While the law requires that all children receive a full-time education from the term after their fifth birthday, you are quite at liberty to provide this education at home until you feel that your child is ready for school (see Chapter 10).

If you are happy that your child is ready to move on into the school environment, however, how can you go about choosing the right primary school for her? This can be more complicated than it may seem, because your choice of secondary school needs to be taken into account, even at this early stage in your child's school career. There are two reasons for this:

- Secondary schools' admissions policies often favour children from particular 'feeder' primary schools.
- The transition from primary to secondary school can be very much easier for your child if many of her classmates are going with her.

Of course, secondary schools can change a good deal over the six years or so that your child will spend in primary school, and I am not suggesting that your choice of primary school should be based solely on your choice of secondary school. In areas where there is fierce competition to get into a particular secondary school, however, it is worth finding out whether the school's admissions policy favours certain primary schools, as this may be a factor in your decision.

Types of school

Before you can begin to choose a school (or schools) for your child, it is helpful to know the difference between the various kinds of school that may be available in your area. Should you choose state or private, single-sex or co-educational? Below is a rough guide to the most common types of school in the UK.

State schools

State schools do not charge fees to parents. In most areas children aged 5 to 10 attend primary schools, and move on to comprehensive secondary schools at 11 for education up to the age of 16 or beyond. In a few areas the middle school system still exists. Here children will start in a first school at 5, move to a middle school at 9, and are then selected by means of an examination at 12 to determine whether they will go on to grammar or secondary modern school.

State schools operate under the auspices of the local education authority, which may also own the school itself. Some are owned by either a charitable foundation or the school's governing body. These technicalities make little difference to pupils and parents, except in that whoever runs the school makes the decisions on admissions. Hence in a voluntary controlled school, the LEA will decide who is admitted, while in a voluntary aided school the governing body will make the decisions. Each school's prospectus will include details of how it is managed and run.

There are two types of state school that differ from regular schools:

- *Specialist schools* (only in England): These secondary schools include technology colleges, language colleges, sports colleges and arts colleges. They will develop a strength in a particular subject area, often in partnership with an employer, but should still, according to the DfES, 'deliver a broad and balanced education through the National Curriculum'.
- *Special schools*: Provided by LEAs for children with certain special educational needs, although the government's inclusion policy requires as many as possible to be educated in ordinary schools.

Selection

Some state secondary schools are wholly or partly selective.

- *Grammar schools* select their pupils wholly on the results of a test sat during the last year of primary school.
- *Partially selective schools* select some of their pupils by overall ability, or by aptitude for a specialist subject, e.g. sport, art, etc.
- Some *comprehensive schools* use banding to ensure that their new intake has a spread of all levels of ability. All children applying are tested, and places are allocated to a predetermined number of children in each ability band.

Independent schools

Independent schools are not funded by the state and often have charitable status. Their income derives largely from fees paid by parents. These schools are inspected to ensure they maintain acceptable standards of premises, accommodation, teaching and staffing, and boarding schools are also inspected by local Social Services departments to ensure that welfare standards are met.

Some independent schools, such as the Parents National Education Union (PNEU), Small Schools or Steiner Schools, are founded on particular educational philosophies or religious beliefs, and will attract parents who adhere to these principles. Others simply offer an alternative to the state school.

State vs independent

Over 90 per cent of schoolchildren in the UK attend state schools, but for those who can afford to pay, some independent schools may offer certain advantages, such as:

- smaller classes;
- better facilities and resources;
- freedom from the restrictions of the National Curriculum;
- specialization in particular areas, e.g. music or ballet schools and those catering for certain disabilities;
- extensive extra-curricular activities;
- boarding facilities.

Many senior independent schools and a few junior schools offer scholarships to attract bright or talented pupils to the school. They are usually awarded after a competitive examination, for academic, musical or artistic merit. Scholarships vary in value but rarely cover the whole fee. Many schools also have bursaries – grants from the school – to help parents to pay the fees. These are often awarded after a 'means test' of family income.

Bear in mind, though, that fees are not the only costs a private education is likely to incur. The uniform and equipment required by a private school can be very expensive, and the costs of school trips and other activities can also be much higher than those a state school would consider reasonable or acceptable. The stresses imposed on parents by finding the funds needed to keep their child in an independent school can sometimes outweigh any benefits of a private education.

Single-sex vs co-educational

Primary schools usually have both girls and boys as pupils. Secondary schools may be either single-sex or co-educational. In many areas, the choice between single-sex and co-educational schools will not be available, but where there is a choice, which offers the better education for your child?

Academic achievement

Research has shown that girls tend to do better academically in a single-sex environment, while boys do better in co-educational schools. It is thought that the earlier maturity of girls, and their tendency to be more self-motivated than boys, is probably responsible for this difference. In other words, girls do better without boys to distract them from their work, while boys benefit from the influence of the more mature girls studying alongside them.

While this is a reasonable assumption, the resulting differential in academic achievement is only an overall tendency. It would not be true to say that all boys do better in a co-educational environment than they would in a single-sex school, or that all girls will achieve more of their academic potential if they are educated separately from boys.

Bullying

It used to be generally accepted that boys bullied more than girls. In fact recent research found that in two single-sex comprehensive schools in London the same percentage of children – some two-thirds of each school's pupils – had experienced bullying as either victim or bully at both the girls' and boys' school.

Is your child more or less likely to be bullied at a single-sex school? What data there is indicates that a co-educational environment is safer for both boys and girls. Some researchers have concluded that the presence of the opposite sex has a moderating influence on the behaviour of both – bullying behaviour is seen as downright unattractive, and both boys and girls care enough about the opinions of others to want to avoid this. A single-sex school with a well-defined and rigorously observed policy on bullying, however, may well be a better bet than a mixed school with a haphazard approach or none at all.

Choosing a primary or secondary school

There are lots of factors involved in choosing a primary or secondary school, but they all boil down to this: which school is right for your child? No one knows your child as well as you, and however happy someone else's child may be at a particular school, your child may be happier somewhere else. It is, therefore, vitally important that you put in some legwork and actually go and see schools in action. First, though, you will need to gather information about all the schools that are available in your area. Your local authority can provide you with a list which will tell you:

- what pupils the schools admit;
- their admission arrangements;
- how popular they are;
- where to get more information.

Once you have identified the schools that you are interested in, you can apply direct to these schools for more detailed information.

What information can you expect from the school?

Every primary and secondary school is required to produce a brochure, or prospectus, which will describe the school's admission policy and procedure, and give you a great deal of information about the way the school is organized and run. This should help to give you a 'feel' for the school, and whether it might suit your individual child.

In addition to this prospectus, every school's governing body is required to produce written policies covering the following areas:

- teaching and learning;
- the organization and management of the school;
- issues to do with behaviour;
- issues of equal opportunity;
- special educational needs;
- use of resources;
- staff pay and conditions;
- buildings and fabric maintenance.

These policies should be readily available at the school for everyone to see, and you can ask for a copy of any policy you are particularly interested in. For instance, you might want to see what the school's policy on bullying is, or how it plans to provide for children with special educational needs.

See for yourself

Some primary and most secondary schools hold open days or evenings, when prospective parents and pupils can look around the school. Each class or department will stage a presentation and/or demonstration of the work of its pupils, and often there will be a talk by the head teacher, teas in the school hall, and so on.

These events can be useful, and give you a chance to see the inside of the buildings and meet members of staff and selected pupils. However, they will give you more of an insight into the organizational and marketing skills of the head teacher and department heads than how it feels to be a pupil there. If you really want to know what the school is like, make an appointment to visit on a normal school day – there should be no objection to this.

While you're at the school, look out for the following:

- How do children treat each other in the corridors and playground, where there is little direct supervision?
- Is there a generally happy and industrious atmosphere?
- Is there lots of the children's work on display?
- Does the school seem to have good resources – plenty of equipment, sports and music facilities, a good library, etc.?
- Does it look cared-for?
- Would your child fit in and be happy here?

Don't forget to ask how the school involves parents, both in their children's education and more generally in the running of the school.

If you can, talk to parents who already have a child at the school you are interested in. For a true 'warts and all' view, though, it's best to talk to the children themselves. No school can please all of the pupils (or parents) all of the time, so don't expect unmitigated praise. Your best indication of the quality of the school will be from the sort of complaints parents and pupils have, and how the school has handled problems in the past.

Parent–Teacher Associations (PTAs, PFTAs, etc.)

Many schools have parent–teacher associations (PTAs). If you don't know anyone with children at the school you are interested in, you can ask the school to put you in touch with someone on the PTA, who will be able to give you inside information on its strengths and weaknesses, and may be able to offer help with the admissions procedure.

OFSTED reports

All schools in England that are wholly or mainly state funded are inspected by the Office for Standards in Education (OFSTED), a government body set up to 'improve standards of achievement and quality of education through regular independent inspection, public reporting and informed independent advice'. Independent schools that are not members of the Independent Schools Council (ISC) are also subject to OFSTED inspections. The ISC has its own inspection system for its member schools. Schools are inspected, on average, every four years – more often if problems have been identified, and less often if the school has been seen as particularly successful in earlier inspections.

This means that an OFSTED report is available for every state school and many independent schools in England. Parents can get the OFSTED report for any school they are interested in from the OFSTED web site, or ask the school itself to show them their report, which should provide the following information:

- *What sort of school it is*: Its quality, strengths and weaknesses, and an evaluation of any changes since the last inspection.
- *How high its standards are*: Examination and test results, trends in performance, an analysis of whether, in the view of the inspectors, pupils in the school are getting on as well as they should. Pupils' attitudes, values and personal development will also be reported.
- *How well pupils are taught*: The quality of teaching and learning, curricular and other opportunities offered to pupils, care of pupils and how well the school works in partnership with parents.
- *How well the school is led and managed*: The management of performance, the role of governors and the school's own monitoring and evaluation.

These can make interesting reading, but you should bear in mind that the current OFSTED report for the school you are interested in can be four years or more out of date, and considerable changes may have taken place, including changes of head teacher and teaching staff, since it was published.

School performance tables

Every year the DfES publishes performance tables for primary and secondary schools. These tables will give you a little background information about the school – chiefly how many children are on the register and how many have special educational needs – and give information about test and examination results. For secondary schools, information about the pupils' absence record is also included.

These tables give a rough guide to how well schools are doing, but they need to be interpreted in the light of the special circumstances that may affect the individual school. For instance, a secondary school that has a high number of pupils for whom English is not their first language may do very well to achieve a GCSE pass rate that would be interpreted as low for a school without this disadvantage. Performance tables, therefore, should not be seen as a definitive guide to the quality of teaching that the school provides.

Policy on bullying

The issue of bullying is often, and quite rightly, a special concern for parents. It's important, therefore, that part of the information you obtain from a prospective school for your child relates to its policy on bullying.

Any staff member at the school, and any child for that matter, should be able to tell you exactly what the school's policy is regarding bullying, and what the school does on a regular basis to reinforce that policy. Examples of effective action might include:

- Assessment of the problem within the school by means of a questionnaire for pupils.
- Established and written policy on bullying, familiar to all staff members and pupils.
- School contract laying down rules of behaviour, contributed to and voted in by pupils, and signed by everyone.
- Regular exposure of the issue in personal and social education, (PSE) and assemblies, through drama, class discussion, and in other ways.
- Written code of conduct issued to all children on a regular basis.
- Clearly defined procedure for reporting bullying to staff, known to all the children and regularly discussed.
- Involvement of parents in the school's dealings with bullies and victims when an incident has been reported.
- Training in prevention and recognition for staff.
- Special measures to protect new intake from older children, e.g. separate playground or playtimes.

- Timetabling to avoid 'rush hour' problems, where large numbers of children move around the school at the same time.
- Institution of 'bully courts'.

If whoever interviews prospective pupils and parents doesn't seem clear about the school's anti-bullying measures, then they are probably not effective. A school that has not thought out and implemented a school-wide policy on bullying is simply not taking the problem seriously enough.

So, you've chosen your school – what next?

Once you know which school you want your child to attend, it is up to you to apply for a place there. In some areas, all the state schools are included on the same form, while in others you must apply separately to each school. Remember that you must fill in a local authority admissions form for any LEA school you want your child to attend, even if it is your second choice and even if you live within its catchment area. If you do not, your child may not be considered for a place until after all those who did apply have been accommodated, and by then there may be no places left at the school of your choice. Attendance at a nursery or infant school linked with an infant or junior school does not guarantee your child a place at that school, so it is important that you ask whether you need to fill in an admissions form in order to secure a place at the school you want.

- You will usually need to apply for a *primary* school place well before your child reaches 5 – many schools admit children at 4.
- You will usually need to apply for a *secondary* place before Christmas in the year before your child is due to start at secondary school.

Oversubscription

You've chosen the school that you feel would best suit your child, but what if everyone else has chosen it too? There are only a limited number of places in any school, so how can you give your child the best possible chance of getting a place?

The information provided by the LEA and the school's own prospectus should tell you whether there were more applications for places in the school in the previous year than there were places available. If so, there are some measures you can take that will give your application a better chance of success.

The rules by which applications are decided must also be published in the school's prospectus and the LEA's booklet, and a careful reading of these will give you some useful clues. They may include:

- whether you live in the school's catchment area;
- whether you have other children already at the school;
- whether your child goes to a nursery or primary school linked to your chosen school (sometimes called a 'feeder school');
- whether your family attends a church to which the school is linked, or one of a particular faith;
- whether there are medical or social reasons that make this the best school for your child.

The relative importance of these rules should be clearly stated. If 'siblings at the school already' is the most important, places should be offered first to all those who have brothers and sisters already attending the school, before moving on to those who qualify through the second rule. You can gain some idea from this hierarchy of how likely your child is to gain a place at this school. This can be very important, because many schools give priority to parents who make their school their first choice. If you waste your first choice on a school that your child has little chance of getting into, you may find that your application is rejected by your second-choice school because you did not choose them first!

In some areas getting your child into the most popular school can become a tactical challenge spread over several years. Some families move house or start attending church in order to get their children into the school of their choice. If you are really confused, try asking advice from your local authority or the school to which you are applying.

What if your child is not offered a place at the school of your choice?

Your LEA must, by law, offer your child a place at a school within reasonable travelling distance. Most children are offered places at their parents' preferred school, but in some areas there is fierce competition for places in the most popular school, and it is inevitable that some of those who apply for the limited number of places available will not be successful. In this case, a place at the second-choice school will usually be offered, but sometimes even this may not be available, and a place will then be offered at a different school.

If you are not happy with the place your child has been offered, you have a right to appeal to an independent panel against the decision. The letter telling you that your application has been unsuccessful will tell you how to appeal, and will give you a time limit within which your appeal must be made.

Appeal procedure

If you decide to appeal against the refusal of your application for a place at your chosen school, the matter will be decided by an independent panel. First, the panel hears the admission authority's case. If it decides that the admission authority was wrong to refuse admission to your child, the panel will reverse the decision and your child will be offered a place. If it decides that the admission authority had good reason to refuse a place, it will move on to hear your case.

You will need to put before them all the reasons why this school would be the best for your child. The panel will then weigh the benefits to your child against the effect that admitting an extra child would have on the school and its other pupils. If the panel decides that the benefits outweigh the disadvantages, it will uphold your appeal and your child will be admitted to the school.

If your admission application has been refused because the school has reached the legal limit for class size, the panel will reverse the admission authority's decision only if it has broken its own rules of admission, or has misrepresented the facts, e.g. the number of pupils at the school or the number of classrooms.

If your appeal fails, you can still ask the school to put your child on their waiting list – places do sometimes come up after the start of term. Of course, this will mean that your child has to start at another school in the meantime, unless you choose to educate her at home, and if it is a popular school it is quite likely that others will be on the waiting list too. All in all, it makes sense to make your first choice a school that your child has a reasonable chance of getting into, as the appeals procedure can be lengthy, and stressful for all concerned.

For more information about appeals, contact the admission authority for the school, or the School Admissions Teams at the DfES.

2

Communicating with the School

Contacting the teacher

Your first point of contact with the school will always be your child's teacher or form tutor. Ideally, you should aim to establish a good relationship with your child's teacher from the start, before you have any concerns to share. A teacher who knows you are interested in your child's time at school is more likely to contact you if there is anything she feels you should know about.

Primary school

It is relatively easy to get to know your child's primary schoolteacher. You will probably see her every day when you drop your child off at school and fetch her at the end of the day, and although most teachers will not have time to stop and chat with parents then, you will at least be able to recognize each other and can exchange a few words if there is anything urgent to be communicated. If an issue arises that you need to talk to your child's primary school teacher about, what should you do? There are several options:

- *A quick chat at the start of the school day*
  If your child has lost her book bag, seems a bit off colour but is not ill enough to keep at home, or has a minor worry about something that will happen at school that day, a few words to the teacher (or classroom assistant) is probably the best approach. Bear in mind, though, that this is the teacher's busiest time – she is preparing for the day's activities, settling in the children as they arrive and probably dealing with requests for attention and information from several parents into the bargain. Be friendly, but keep to the point and make it snappy.

21

- *A note*

  If someone different will be collecting your child from school, or she has a twisted ankle and mustn't take part in PE, a brief note to the teacher is probably best. These are not matters that require discussion, but the teacher needs to remember them, and will appreciate a reminder that she can put in the register or keep on her desk. This approach also works for anything that you would like to tell your teacher about, but don't want to discuss in front of a classroom full of parents and children – or your own child. Children are not immune to embarrassment.

- *A telephone call*

  If you can't get into school, you can telephone and ask to talk to your child's teacher. It's not likely that she will be able to speak to you there and then, but most teachers will be happy to call you back when they are free.

- *A request for an appointment*

  If you need to discuss something with your child's teacher – her progress, worries about bullying or family circumstances that might affect her performance at school, for instance – it is best to make an appointment to talk to her teacher after school. Once the school day has ended, the teacher will be able to give you her full attention and as much time as it takes to talk the matter over. You can ask for an appointment when you drop off or collect your child, or you could write a note or telephone your request. In either case, it is wise to give an idea of what you want to discuss, so that the teacher can talk to other staff members and children if necessary, and can gauge roughly how long the discussion is likely to take.

If your child is bussed to school, communication is not quite so easy, and you will have to rely on notes, telephone calls and appointments to keep in touch. If it is at all possible, try to take your child to school yourself at least once a week for her first term. This will really help you to establish communication with her teacher, and to talk to your child about school and what happens there.

Secondary school

When your child starts secondary school, communication with teachers suddenly gets much more difficult. For a start, there are now so many of them – most secondary schoolchildren will have different teachers for every subject, and these teachers will probably see each child for only an hour or two a week, at most. Some teachers will teach up to 500 different children in a week, so it would be quite unrealistic to expect that every subject teacher will even remember who your child is, let alone be able to tell you very much about how she gets on in their lessons, beyond what marks she gets.

Form tutors, however, will have the opportunity to get to know the children in their class a little better. If you have a concern about your child's general progress or happiness at school, it is to the form tutor that you should turn first. Even if your concern is over a particular subject, it is wise to make the form tutor your first port of call, as she needs to maintain an overview of your child's school experience – she will be able either to pass you on to the relevant subject teacher or to act as a go-between.

Building a relationship with your child's form tutor isn't easy. Unless you make an appointment to see her for some reason, your first meeting is likely to be at a parents' evening, when she will have five or ten minutes to prove to you that she knows who your child is, and to answer any questions you may have. (See p. 27 for tips on using this time wisely.) If you need to communicate with her between parents' evenings, there are several ways of going about it:

- *A note*

  As with the primary schoolchild, this approach works for issues that need no discussion – an explanation that your child's school shoes are at the menders, a warning that she may be upset because the family dog has died, etc. Some schools provide children with a notebook to be used for communications between home and school. This has the advantage that the teacher will sign the page to show that your note has been read, but obviously you will not want to use it for any messages that you don't want your child, or other children, to read.

23

- *A telephone call*
  If you need to ask your child's tutor something, or to discuss a concern (fairly briefly), a telephone call to the school is the best approach. The teacher will probably not be available there and then, but will usually call you back at a mutually convenient time. This can be helpful if you are at work and can't get away to meet the teacher during the school day.
- *An appointment*
  For issues that can't be resolved quickly over the telephone, make an appointment to see your child's tutor. Usually you can do this by sending in a note or by telephoning the school's receptionist/secretary.

Reports

The content and frequency of reports varies tremendously from school to school, but you can expect to get at least one report per school year, usually towards the end of the summer term. The report will contain:

- comments on progress in all subjects;
- comments on general progress as part of the school community;
- an attendance record;
- at the end of key stages, a summary of your child's and the school's SATS results, and national results for comparison.

The amount of information that is presented in school reports is variable, and a matter of school policy. Some reports will be composed almost entirely of standard phrases relating to the learning targets set for that age group, and will tell you what your child has learned, rather than how well, easily or happily he has learnt it. Some teachers will have used a computer programme providing a database of comments that can be added automatically to the blank report, but many will have taken considerable trouble to say something personal about each child. It is always encouraging to read comments that show that the writer actually knows who he is talking about, but we have to accept that, at

24

secondary school at least and in the state sector, many teachers never get the chance to know very much at all about the individual children they teach.

Primary school

A primary school report will usually comprise general comments on your child's progress in the various areas she is studying under the National Curriculum. Grades are not usually awarded at this stage, but your child's teacher and head teacher may write at some length about how well she is fitting into the school, her attitude to her work and what she is like to teach.

Secondary school

Secondary school reports will usually include grades in all subjects, typically awarded for various aspects of your child's attainment, according to the subject. In mathematics, for example, your child may be graded for effort; using and applying maths; number and algebra; shape, space and measures; handling data and mental strategies. These grades will give you a rough guide to how well your child is doing academically, but they do need to be interpreted carefully. As any child will tell you, some teachers are easier markers than others, and a B from one teacher may be equal to an A from another who awards grades more generously. More important than the grades themselves are the trends that become apparent over time. For instance, if your child has regularly achieved Bs in maths, and a report arrives that shows mostly Cs in this subject, you will need to find out from his maths teacher why he feels your child's grades have changed. For this reason, it is helpful to have reports on your child more frequently than once a year, so that any problems can be spotted and tackled early.

The report will include the results of any tests your child has taken, and possibly also set targets for him to work towards. There should be some comments from each teacher on your child's general progress and what he is like to teach, and comments from his form tutor, head of year and head teacher.

COMMUNICATING WITH THE SCHOOL

Talking to your child about his report

You will probably read your child's report for the first time in his presence. He will already have had the opportunity, at most schools, to see its contents, and unless he has done exceptionally well he will probably be very anxious about at least some of the entries. As we will see in Chapter 4, his confidence in his own ability and in your belief in him is vital if your child is to make the most of his opportunities in life. As you read the report, try to keep this in mind and praise him whenever you read a favourable comment or see good (or improved) grades. Don't discount subjects like technology or PE as 'not proper subjects' – if your child has done well in these give him the credit he is due. If some results are disappointing, don't say too much at this stage.

Having read the report through once, go through it again, more carefully, with your child. Talk about each subject, what he likes and dislikes about it, what the teacher is like, whether he thinks the grades and comments are a fair reflection of his achievement. If he feels that an entry completely misrepresents his achievement in that subject, make a note to ask the teacher about it at the parents' evening – it is not unknown for teachers to make mistakes, and it can be a great disincentive for a child to have his year's work marked down because he has been mistaken for another child.

Where grades are lower than you expected or would like, talk to your child about why he feels he is not doing very well in that subject. Try to do this constructively, and be aware that not everyone can achieve straight As. The object is to help your child to do the best of which he is capable, and a comparatively low grade in some subjects may represent a big effort for the child who is not naturally gifted in that direction. Remember to praise him for any improvement on his last report, however slight.

Next, look at the overall picture: is he scoring consistently low grades for effort or homework, for example? Talk to your child about why he thinks that might be the case, and what would make those areas easier for him. Is he happy at school generally? Is anything worrying him? You should come out of this discussion process with a good idea of your child's strengths and weaknesses, and a list of points to discuss with his teachers at the parents' evening. Your child should come out of it knowing that his efforts have been recognized and appreciated, and that further improvement in areas where he is underachieving (if he is) will also be recognized and appreciated. He should be confident that you understand any problems he is having at school, and you will discuss them with his teachers and help him to overcome them. You should both have a clear idea about what practical help he can expect from you, and above all he should be able to face the next school year (or term) with confidence in his own ability and the ability of his teachers and parents to work together to help him achieve his potential.

Parents' evenings

Both primary and secondary schools will offer parents the chance to talk to their child's teacher/s, usually after receiving their annual report. Teachers dread these occasions – they come at the end of a long school day, time is limited and they must face critical comments from parents who often cannot believe that their child could possibly do any wrong. In many cases, however, this is the only contact you will have with your child's teachers. How can you use this time to your child's best advantage?

Read the report

Identify any areas where your child appears to be having difficulties, or is not achieving as much as you think she could be. Make a note of these, and ask to see the teacher concerned.

Look at the work

You will probably have seen some of your primary schoolchild's work already, as children generally love to show off their achievements. At parents' evenings, her work may be laid out for you to look at as you wait for your appointment, so try to arrive a bit early and take this opportunity to look through any books you have not seen.

At secondary schools, your child's work is generally not available to view at parents' evenings. Since secondary school-children bring their books home with them (unless they are with a teacher being marked) you can ask to see her books at home. Look for the general standard of work, the marks and grades awarded and whether or not her work has been marked consistently and recently.

Finding a great deal of unmarked work in your child's books is a cause for concern, and you should ask the relevant teacher about it, although there is often a perfectly reasonable explanation. Bear in mind that some of the work in your child's books may be notes copied from the blackboard or dictated by the teacher. This will not be graded. If you are in doubt, ask your child. Again, make a note of everything you notice that you would like your child's teacher to explain.

Start on the right foot

Even if you have concerns about your child's work or the way that a particular teacher is teaching her, start your interview by shaking hands and saying hello pleasantly. This may seem obvious, but we all carry around with us memories of our own schooldays, and teachers can sometimes seem like threatening authority figures. This can make us feel defensive and act aggressively. It is much less likely that you will get the outcome you want from a discussion with a teacher if you put him on the defensive from the start.

Ask your questions

Go armed with a list of the questions you want to ask, and don't be ashamed to refer to it. The teacher will be glad that you are taking the interview seriously, and have some questions for him to answer. It relieves the pressure on him to think of something new to say about your child.

Listen to the answers

Having asked your questions, listen carefully to the teacher's answers. If you disagree with his assessment of your child, wait until he has finished speaking, and then put your point of view.

Although time is limited, it is important that topics are not rushed and left incomplete.

Be constructive

If you feel that the school or the individual teacher is failing your child in some way, try not to make the interview a personal attack on the teacher. 'I'm worried about Sally's grades in English – she started well but her grades have slipped this term. I'd like to find some way of helping her to improve,' will gain much better results than, 'I'm disgusted that Sally has gone from a B to a D in English since you started teaching her. It's not good enough, and if something isn't done about it I will seriously consider changing schools.'

Say thank you

Make it a practice to thank each teacher for what they have done for your child. If she is doing well, don't be afraid to make an appointment with a teacher at parents' evening just to say so – teachers often feel that they only hear from parents when things are going wrong, and a bit of praise will go a long way in terms of job satisfaction. It may also, of course, make that teacher just a bit more committed to your child's welfare and progress, and any advantage you can give your child has to be worth a few words of encouragement once a year!

Questions to ask

Your child's teacher may well have things he wants to say to you, and there will probably be questions arising from his report that you will want to cover. If not, here are some questions you might want to ask.

Of a primary teacher or class tutor:
- Does my child seem happy at school?
- Is he making and keeping friends?
- Is his behaviour good?

Of any teacher:
- Has my child made sufficient progress since his last report
- What are his strengths?
- What is he finding difficult? How can I help him in these areas?
- Does he try hard enough?
- Does he join in class discussions and activities?
- How can I help with his schoolwork in general?

The appointment system

Most schools have an appointment system for parents' evenings, allowing five or ten minutes with each teacher. You will be able to book an appointment in advance at a time to suit you, although you may find that all a given teacher's appointments have been booked and you cannot be seen. If this is the case and you want to see that teacher, if only to find out what they're like, you should be able to make an appointment with them at another time.

Some schools ask you to come without your child. It may be that you want to discuss your child's progress, or factors outside school that may affect it, without your child hearing, particularly with a primary-age child, but for secondary-age children and many younger ones, it can be very helpful to have them in on the discussion. If they are doing well, they can gain great confidence from having their parents told so by their teachers in their presence. If there are areas where they can improve, it can be very useful for them to agree targets together with teacher and parents, to which everyone can help them work. If issues arise that need more discussion than the 5–10 minute slot allows, ask for an appointment to discuss them further rather than rush through them with the next set of parents breathing down your neck.

When to raise issues between meetings, when to wait

You will get the chance at parents' evenings to raise any concerns you may have about your child, but this may happen only once a year. When should you contact the school between times? If you have any concerns about your child that can't be covered in a brief exchange with her teacher, it is always better to talk about them sooner rather than later. These worries might include:

- problems with school work;
- other problems at school (e.g. bullying);
- problems at home that might affect your child at school (e.g. marital problems, illness in the family, moving house);
- concerns about an aspect of your child's behaviour or learning that you think may need expert help.

All these issues, and many more, need to be discussed with your child's teacher as soon as possible. Some parents feel reluctant to waste teachers' time. Teachers are, indeed, very busy people and have a long and stressful working day, but they are also concerned to do the best they can for their pupils, and no teacher worth his salt would begrudge half an hour of his time to talk over a situation that could affect one of his pupils' learning potential.

Helping in school

One way to get to know your child's teacher, and to become more familiar with what happens in school, is to offer to help out.

Primary school

Most primary schools welcome parents' help with special activities like cooking, crafts, swimming or trips, or with day-to-day tasks like hearing the children read. Any training that is necessary will be given by the school, and the only qualification you will need is to enjoy being with children and have a well-developed sense of humour.

Working with your own child's class can be very interesting, and sometimes children at school are quite different from the child we know at home. For some children, however, having a parent around can be difficult. This is particularly true for the rather clingy child who may have found his feet in school, but feels that as long as Mum is there he has to stay close to her. If this is the case for your child, and it doesn't wear off after a few sessions, you can still ask to help with another class. Spending time in school will help you to understand your child's world, and give you an insight into any worries he brings home.

If you have a younger child, many primary schools will be happy for you to bring her into the classroom while you hear reading, for example. Some, however, may feel that a toddler could prove disruptive. If you do take your younger child into school with you, be aware of the effect she is having on the class. If it is a problem, you may have to give up for the time being and return when she is a little older.

For those parents who don't want to commit themselves to helping on a regular basis, annual events like sports day and the school fête offer the opportunity for one-off involvement, and the chance to meet other parents and staff out of school.

Secondary school

Secondary schools generally have far less parent involvement in the school day. Some parents may be welcomed to help with certain specific activities, particularly during activities weeks, sports days and other events where children are taking part in extra-curricular activities. Help will be needed with trips, and with school fund-raising activities, usually organized by the parent–teacher association (or its equivalent).

Workshops for parents

Some primary and secondary schools hold special workshops for parents, designed to show them what their children are doing at school. These events will usually concentrate on individual subjects, like maths or reading. Since teaching methods and the subjects that children are taught have changed considerably since most parents were at school, this sort of event can give a useful insight into our children's school experiences, as well as enabling parents and teachers to get to know one another in more relaxed circumstances than the average parents' evening.

Parents' associations

Parents' associations (PTA, PTFA, Friends of . . . , etc.) provide an opportunity for parents who want to be involved with their child's education, but not necessarily help in the classroom, perhaps because they work during the school day, to become more closely involved with the school.

The National Council of Parent–Teacher Associations defines a parents' association as 'a group of parents who are working together with the school to achieve the best for all concerned'. Fund-raising for the school will be a large part of this, but parents' associations also provide a means of communication between school staff and parents, and can have input into decisions on school policies. PTA members often go on to become classroom assistants or parent governors.

Joining the PTA is the best way to become involved with your child's secondary school. When help is needed with events like open evenings, or in the library, or to run the school uniform shop, this is where school staff will go to find it. If you have the time and energy, you can volunteer to sit on the committees organizing individual events or looking at specific issues that affect the school. Alternatively you can simply make yourself available on a one-off basis to help out with events on the day.

School governors

Every school has a governing body, a committee made up of elected and co-opted representatives of the staff, the LEA, parents, support staff and, often, the local church, charitable trust or business.

The governing body is responsible for ensuring that the school provides a good-quality education. They are not responsible for the day-to-day running of the school, which is the head teacher's job, but make decisions on policy, staffing and sometimes admissions. Complaints about the school and its staff that the head teacher cannot settle will be passed on to the governing body.

Parent governors are elected by other parents at the school, and have exactly the same standing on the governing body as the other representatives. If you want to be involved in policy-making at your child's school, and have time and energy to spare, standing for election as a parent governor could be for you. You need to be prepared to attend one or two meetings a term – more if you are on a committee looking at a specific aspect of the school.

The governors' report

Once a year, the governing body will issue a report to parents, following which an annual parents' meeting will be held. This report will include information on the school's finances, progress made towards OFSTED recommendations, test and exam results, staff and training, and many other aspects of the school's year. It will also contain details of action taken following resolutions passed at the last annual meeting, and of the next election of parent governors.

Attendance at the annual meeting can be a very useful way of raising general concerns about the school that have not been addressed satisfactorily by the head teacher or governors.

Teachers are people too

I spoke to many teachers in the course of my research for this book, and the one thing that almost every one of them said, in one way or another, was: 'Tell parents that teachers are people too.' Perhaps because of the way we as children all saw teachers, we tend to forget, rather as we do with our own parents, that they are just ordinary human beings like the rest of us. Perhaps we would rather that they weren't. We must trust them with our most precious 'possessions', our children, and we very much want to believe that they are infallible, impartial and always at their best. Of course, they aren't, any more than the rest of us.

Try to remember, when you judge your child's teacher, that she too has arguments with her spouse, money and health worries, problems with her own children, and all the other distractions that every one of us has to face in our own lives. She arrives early at school, often after a late night preparing work for the next day, to a demanding and stressful job often made more so by large classes and a lack of resources. The vast majority really want to do the best for their pupils but, while we are entitled to expect a very high standard of professionalism from our teachers, they will inevitably sometimes fall a little short of the mark. One mistake doesn't make a bad teacher, and you can be pretty certain that she knows that she has slipped up and feels as bad about it as you do. Here is a heartfelt plea from Raymond, a semi-retired primary teacher with some 20 years' experience:

Have the maturity and wisdom to accept that your child is not perfect. Also, be prepared to accept that children often behave differently at school from the way they do at home. Have the humility to understand that there are NO perfect parents – which includes yourself. It may be that some of your parenting skills need examining. Smile at your child's teacher and acknowledge them whenever possible. Find every excuse and reason to praise them and thank them for what they do. Sincere praise and gratitude will lift the teacher's heart and he/she will walk on air for a while. This can only benefit your child!

3

Expectations and Motivation

Why do you want your child to do well at school?

If asked, most parents would say they wanted their child to do well at school so that he could get a good and fulfilling job, and have a comfortable and successful life as an adult. For the child whose heart is set upon becoming a doctor or a lawyer, education is obviously crucial in the achievement of his ambitions. The days have gone, however, when a university degree assured its holder of a good job, or indeed any job at all, and many people still have satisfying and fulfilling careers without academic qualifications.

It is very likely that your child will one day ask you, 'But why should I work hard and do well at school?' Before this happens, it is a good idea to examine your reasons for wanting your child's academic success, and to allow for the possibility that striving for academic achievement may not be the best course for every child, and perhaps not for yours.

What's in it for you?

Our children represent the biggest investment of our lives, in terms of love, time and (let's face it) money. Not only do we want the best for them, but what they achieve contributes to our feelings of success or failure as parents. This is perfectly understandable – parenting is a hard job to which we devote many years of our lives, and there is little recognition for it. We all want to be well thought of by others and to feel good about our own achievements, and our children's educational successes are often our only public proof that we have made a good job of it.

What's in it for your child?

There are certain common crisis points in a child's educational career when he is most likely to question the assumption that academic success is important for him.

Starting school

Young children may see no reason for going to school when they are perfectly happy at home and sure that they will want to be there for the rest of their lives. Once their relationships with their teachers are established, the desire to please them and their parents will be enough to motivate most children to do well.

Teenage rebellion

The desire to please teachers can become less pressing in secondary school, where the relationship between teacher and individual pupil is inevitably less close than it was in primary school. This, coupled with the natural assertion of independence that comes with growing up, can leave a motivation gap – now the child needs to find his own reasons for succeeding. The additional pressure of choosing the subjects they want to study for GCSEs, and by implication being asked to decide on their career ambitions, can leave children longing to escape as soon as possible.

Post-16

Many 16-year-olds feel that they have grown out of school, and can't wait to leave. They have a chance, at 16, to make their first big decision about their future, and the short-term benefits of doing so may feel far more pressing than the vague benefit of staying on for another two years in an environment that just doesn't seem to fit any more.

Going to university

A similar crisis hits when the transition from school to university looms. After two years of intense pressure to achieve the A-level grades required, and with three more years of exams ahead, together with facing the trauma of leaving home and adapting to a completely different way of life, some young people may feel overwhelmed by the whole prospect and opt out. The gap year can provide a good solution to this.

Providing motivation

If you want to provide your child with motivation to succeed at school, and are sure that what you are proposing is really the best thing for her as a whole person, you will need to arm yourself with some examples of the benefits to her of your proposed course of action. Let's look at the reasons that you might give your child for doing well at school.

- *Keeping her options open*
  It is important that your child understands that while she may see herself now as a self-employed web site designer, or expect to take over the family business when you retire, circumstances may well change. If she wants to retrain at a later date, but hasn't got the basic qualifications to do so, it can be difficult, expensive and time-consuming to catch up. You may not be able to support her while she does it.
- *Changing her mind*
  She won't be wearing the same clothes or listening to the same music in 15 years' time, and she might not want to do the same job or have the same interests either. She may one day want to follow a different path, whether this means a change of job or a course of study, and a set of basic qualifications will enable her to do this.
- *Building self-esteem*
  Quite apart from the practical considerations, sticking at things and doing them well, even if we can't see any immediate benefit from them, goes a long way towards making us feel good about ourselves, and building the confidence we need to tackle important challenges. How will she feel about herself if she gives up now?
- *Broadening her outlook on life*
  Education isn't just about work. Although some subjects

39

appear to have little practical relevance (religious education or history, for example), they do help us to understand the world we live in and the people around us, and that brings all sorts of very tangible benefits in our working and personal lives.

- *This is just a bad patch – you'll feel better about it later*
  When your child is going through a bad patch – particularly as exams approach but also when things in her personal life aren't going too well – it can help to reassure her that you have felt just the same, and that she will feel much better once the immediate pressure has eased. Planning a holiday or outing for the future can help, as can providing a 'day off' at the time.

- *Learning is fun*
  Gaining knowledge can be an exciting and stimulating activity in itself. Show your child that this is so by taking an interest in the subjects she is studying, and asking her to explain things to you. Sharing her newly-acquired knowledge with someone who takes a keen interest will be a powerful motivation to acquire more, and the thrill of being able to tell your parent something he/she doesn't know should not be underestimated.

- *I wish I'd done better myself*
  By all means tell your child how much you regret not having tried harder at school yourself, and how you feel your life might have been different if you had. Once is probably enough, though – if you make too much of it your child may feel that she is simply being asked to fulfil your fantasies, and rebel. Linking her success to something *she* wants to do will be much more motivating.

- *To please me*
  Children want to gain their parents' approval, and showing her how happy you are when she has tried hard and/or done well will provide a very positive incentive for her to continue. Putting pressure on her to succeed with threats of withdrawing your affection will not work, however, and should be avoided.

- *To impress others*
  'What will people think if you fail/drop out?' is not likely to impress your child as a reason for doing well at school. She probably feels that the people who matter to her – her friends –

don't care much one way or the other, or might even be impressed if she rebelled or dropped out, and doesn't really care what *your* friends think anyway.

- *Your sister did better than this*
  Comparing your child's achievements with another's can be especially damaging, particularly within the family. A high-achieving sibling can be a hard act to follow, and the child who tries hard within her own abilities but is constantly compared with a more academically able brother or sister may feel that she can never win, so she may as well give up. It can be difficult, but try to see each child as an individual and measure them against their own standards.

- *Because I say so*
  The fallback position of the exasperated parent, this really won't wash with most children. If you reach this stage, it is better to end the conversation by saying: 'I think we both need to think seriously about what you can get out of your education. Let's go away and write down everything that we can think of for or against your staying on at school (for instance), and then get back together to discuss it again.'

You know your own child, and despite the temptation to make her feel bad about not doing her best, you will probably be able to find some reason that is meaningful to her for making the effort required to achieve her full educational potential. Motivating your child to do well is not just about what you say, however. The way you feel about school will influence your child's attitudes and perceptions of her own time there.

How was it for you?

Schools have changed radically in less than a generation, and whatever your own experience of school it is likely that your child's will be significantly different. It is important that you examine your own school experiences and understand how schools have changed since you were a pupil, and there are two main reasons for this.

- The more you know about school now, the more you will be able to help your child to benefit from it, and to help him with any problems that arise.
- Any negative feelings you have about school and the experiences you had there could easily influence the way your child sees school.

Most of us don't think about our schooldays much once we are grown up, yet school was our daily environment during some of the most formative years of our lives. For better or worse, what happened there changed us and helped to make us the people we are today. Often we didn't think of our school as particularly bad or good – it was just school, rather as our parents were just our parents. If you had a good experience of school, you will be able to talk about school easily with your child, and he will pick up on your positive feelings about it. If, however, your time at school was particularly unhappy, frustrating or just plain boring, there is a real danger that your child will be affected by your lack of enthusiasm, and that your own dealings with the school will be tainted by your negative feelings. If this is the case, you will need to make a conscious effort to think of your child's school experiences in their own right, and not see them in the light of your own. It may help to think about some of the ways in which schools have changed.

What is school like now?

Of course, some of what happens at school is still routine and, at least to the child, pointless. This is, to some extent, unavoidable in an underfunded and overstretched system. However, many of the problems that were widespread in schools a generation ago have been addressed, with varying degrees of success, by reforms in educational policy and practice.

Boredom

The broad content of your child's education is now governed by the National Curriculum which, while it can't eliminate poor teachers, at least ensures that a broad range of subject matter is covered. There is a wealth of teaching and learning resource material available from the DfES and many other sources, and the growth of the Internet has made this far more accessible for use by teachers and children. The material that is presented to children in school – reading books, worksheets and so on – is constantly improving and becoming more engaging and exciting for children to use.

Bad schools

The much-maligned OFSTED inspections have succeeded in identifying those schools that are performing poorly, and ensuring that resources are targeted at bringing them up to standard as quickly as possible.

Discipline

Teachers are far more accountable than they used to be for the way in which they treat the children in their care. While many would say that this has led to a breakdown in discipline in some schools, it does mean that children need not be afraid of teachers in the way that they sometimes were a generation or so ago. Beatings do not now take place, although sadly some teachers will still use humiliation and verbal bullying to try and control their classes. However, this is no longer considered acceptable and a complaint of this nature should be taken seriously by any head teacher or governing body.

Bullying

Bullying is now universally acknowledged as a serious problem and, although some schools are better than others at tackling it, it should no longer be possible for any school to overlook an incident of bullying that has been brought to its attention.

Accountability

Schools are now obliged to meet certain standards, and parents who don't feel that these targets are being met have recourse to a clear complaints procedure (see Chapter 8).

Relevance

It's true to say that a very great deal of what your child learns in school will never be directly of use to her once she leaves, but many schools are attempting to make what they do more relevant to life outside school. Secondary schools in many areas are forming partnerships with local businesses, in which areas of study of interest to the companies are supported, and work experience and insights into the way industry works are provided for older pupils. Primary and secondary schools often forge links with their local community in an effort to give their pupils a grounding in citizenship, and a feeling of belonging to the community in which they live.

Exams

The modular approach has taken some of the pressure off public examination candidates. In the words of one teacher: 'Where in the real world do you go to work, learn something and then be tested on it in two years' time? You don't. If you're doing a project at work, you do that project, you take it to your managing director, they look at it and evaluate it and they give you a performance rating.' Fortunately, the days of blowing your one chance at an exam pass because you felt a bit off-colour on the day have gone.

Do children enjoy school?

If you ask any child what school is like, his first response is likely to be, 'Boring', or, 'I hate it'. This knee-jerk response, however, actually means very little for most children. If you spend a little time questioning children about what they actually do during the school day, as I have, you will soon be rewarded with glimpses of enthusiasm and excitement.

'The lunches are good!'

'Geography's good – we get to go on field trips.'

'We made a big giant in art. It was good fun designing it and printing onto cloth to make its body.'

'The clubs at lunchtimes are good.'

'I did a talk on horses. I took a bridle and explained how it worked.'

Most children now go happily to school, and enjoy much of the work and play they undertake there.

Gender and motivation

It is generally accepted in the teaching profession that girls are more self-motivated than boys. Of course, this is a trend and will not hold true for every child, but there is concern about the number of underachieving boys, and considerable time and resources have been devoted to trying to rectify this shortfall. This appears to be yielding good results already, and it is likely that the gap will continue to close.

For both boys and girls, there may be academic benefits to be had from a co-educational environment, especially if teachers are aware that they can use gender differences to the benefit of the children. Bob Brewer, a deputy head with 30 years' experience in secondary education, often asks his classes to sit alternately, boy, girl, boy, girl.

> The kids groan but, actually, I notice a huge difference in the behaviour and the work of boys when they're sitting next to a girl. Boys tend to take more risks, they'll jump in without planning; girls plan more, they communicate better, but girls don't take risks. The girls are a good influence on the boys, of course, but actually boys also help girls. A girl might say, 'Oh, let's do it this way', and the boys have said, 'No, that's ordinary. Hey, come on, let's go for this,' and that's helped the girl to look at the problem in a fresh way.

The less well-motivated child of either gender may need help to find more and shorter-term reasons for doing well at school. This can mean more interest and input from parents on a daily basis, looking at school books, helping with homework and talking about what has happened during the school day. The self-motivated child, however, may find this intrusive, so be guided by your observations and those of your child's teachers, and be prepared to revise your attitudes as your child matures.

Be positive

Our school system is not perfect, but it is possible for most children, with the support of their parents, to negotiate the pitfalls and to enjoy and exploit the opportunities it offers them. The key to success is a confident and positive approach, and in the next chapter we will look at general ways in which we can help our children to grow in confidence within the family.

4

Building Confidence

Imagine that you work for a large institution. All your work is monitored and assessed by your superiors and the results are made known to your peers, against whom you are constantly measured. You are subjected to regular tests, and undergo an annual assessment of both your achievements at work and your personal qualities. A copy of this assessment is sent to those closest to you, and they are invited to come to your workplace and discuss you with your managers.

Not many of us would feel entirely comfortable in this situation, and most would probably only stay in such a job if the rewards were very high indeed, yet we send our children off into just such an environment every school day for 13 years, and fondly think of them as the best days of their lives. School can, indeed, be a very positive experience, but we shouldn't underestimate the magnitude of what we are asking our children to do.

School presents our children with a challenge, and any challenge involves the risk of failure. Modern educational methods aim to bring out the best in each child within his capabilities, and there is less overt elitism in education than there was a generation ago, when selection was the norm and some children were pigeonholed from an early age as non-academic, and therefore failures in terms of education. Nevertheless, engaging in a school-based education exposes a child to the risk of failure, from being stuck on the lowest reading book in the class to doing badly in his GCSEs. The confident child whose self-image can take a few knocks will be far better equipped to take these risks than the child for whom a small setback confirms his fears that he is just not good enough.

Building your child's self-confidence from the start

Anyone who has more than one child will know that all children are different, and these differences are manifest almost from the moment of birth. Some babies are more demanding than others, some are easily frightened and wary of strangers, some take on all new challenges and experiences with gusto from a very early age. When we bring up a child, we do not start with a completely blank slate, and part of our job as parents is to recognize the needs of each of our children and tailor our parenting accordingly. Before we begin this fine-tuning, however, there are certain basic needs that must be fulfilled if any baby is to develop into a confident child, capable of taking on the challenge of life and getting the most from the opportunities that present themselves to him.

Love

Your child needs to know that you love her for who she is, not what she does or who she might become. She needs your love to be consistent so that, even if you are feeling very angry with her, you and she both know that you still love her underneath. In a crisis, you need to be able to say, 'I hate what you have done or the way you are behaving, but I still love you.'

Security

Children need to be properly fed and housed, and to have their emotional needs met consistently. A child who is constantly worried that something bad will happen in his life – that his home is not secure or that an emotional catastrophe is about to take place – will find it very difficult to feel positive about himself or the world around him. He will not feel able to add to his problems by responding to challenges and taking risks at school, or anywhere else. It isn't possible to avoid all the ups and downs of life, and family crises may affect many children at some stage in their lives, but we need to be aware of the effect these may have on the child's confidence and do anything we can to help children understand and get over these difficult episodes.

Relationships

Children build up their self-awareness through relationships with their own family, and also with all sorts of people outside the home. The ability to relate to others will be particularly important once they start school, and have to form relationships not only with their peers, but with the adults who teach and look after them. You can help your child to feel at ease with people by introducing her to all sorts of social situations before she starts school – visits to friends, mother-and-toddler groups, outings to the shops and many more – and later by encouraging her to mix with other children and adults outside school. Teaching children to be concerned for the feelings of others, and insisting on basic good manners at home as well as when out in public, will help them to understand and cope with social situations.

Example

Whatever you *say* to your child, what you *do* will be far more likely to influence the way he learns to behave and feels about himself. Telling your child with a slap that hitting another child is wrong, for example, will leave him feeling at best confused, and at worst thinking that hitting is an adult way to respond to frustration and anger. A clear and consistent example will give your child confidence that he understands what is required of him and can meet these expectations.

Because your example is such a powerful influence on your child's life, there is a very real danger that you will pass on your own anxieties to him unwittingly, and for this reason it is important that you spend a little time trying to understand yourself if you want to make as good a parent as possible for your child. If you have hang-ups that you have spent your life so far working around, now is the time to try and sort them out.

Support

Your child needs you to be solidly behind her in whatever she tries to do. She needs to know that you will give her good advice and will always have her best interests at heart. When things go wrong, as they inevitably will from time to time, she needs to know that you will not apportion blame or reject her as a failure, but will help her to find constructive ways of handling the situation.

Rewards

Throughout his childhood, your child needs you to let him know clearly when he has done the right thing, or is moving in the right direction. Tell your child often that you are proud of him and impressed by his achievements, whether he has tied his own shoelace for the first time or had a particularly good school report. Make sure that you notice and acknowledge even the small efforts and improvements. The confidence that this gives your child will enable him to build on them and go on to make bigger ones.

Sometimes we forget how much our approval means to our children. All children, but especially those who are suffering a lapse in self-confidence, can be affected far more than we expect by what we consider a throwaway remark.

I thought I'd done pretty well with my children until a row with my 21-year-old son blew up. Along with a list of other ways in which I'd made his life a misery, he cited the example of his GCSE results, which had been only just good enough to enable him to take the A levels he wanted. He was never a hard worker at school, as all his teachers had pointed out to me at parents' evenings, and I had quite expected him to fail at least some subjects. When he showed me his results, I said, 'Wow, just think how well you could have done if you'd worked!' I meant this as a compliment, as he had obviously passed some subjects on natural ability alone, but apparently he took it as a dreadful insult. Although he didn't mention it at the time, it had obviously played on his mind for five years. I realized then how easy it is to damage your children's self-esteem without really meaning to. I'm certainly more careful now about saying exactly what I mean to my younger children.

Practical ways of helping

Here are some practical ways in which you can help your child to become a confident and happy individual.

Decision-making

If we want our children to have confidence in themselves, we need to show them that we have confidence in them – giving them the opportunity to contribute to decisions about their lives demonstrates this clearly, and also helps children to learn the decision-making skills they will need throughout their adult lives. Very young children can help in the choice of family meal, in choosing their own clothes or the afternoon's activity, for instance. The older child can choose which after-school activities to try or decide how to decorate her bedroom. It is important that you let your child make her own mistakes in these relatively unimportant choices: finding that the dress you desperately wanted because of the floaty overskirt is too tight to walk in comfortably and makes you sweaty on hot days will be a valuable lesson in tempering desire with more practical considerations.

Even in decisions where they cannot be allowed the final say, such as the choice of secondary school, children should be brought in on the decision-making process and their views considered seriously. Remember that your child will be better motivated to do well at a school that she has chosen to attend, or when she at least understands the reasons for her parents' choice.

Be consistent

Children need the security that a consistent set of family rules and values brings. Difficult though it sometimes is, once we have made a rule or demand it is important that we enforce it consistently and see it through to completion, even when this means more work or time wasted for us. If you have told your child to pick up his toys from the living room floor, for instance, it is important that he does so, even if this means half an hour falling over them while he complains and dithers about where they should go.

However much your child complains about what you ask him to do, self-respect is built on fulfilling our obligations and responsibilities in life. The child who is allowed to let things slide will inevitably feel anxious about his worth as a person, and may fail to appreciate that his actions are important, and that what he does or fails to do has consequences, both for himself and others.

Listening

Things that feel really important can be very hard to talk about, but you can only help your child with her problems effectively if you know what they are. If talking about things is the established way of coping in your family, there is a much better chance that your child will turn to you in a crisis. You can encourage this from the start.

- Make some time every day to talk with your child about what she has done and felt. Bath time is a good opportunity to talk to the younger child: 'What did we do today? We went to the shops, didn't we? And what did we buy?' For the school-age child, teatime or bedtime could be your time for going over the day's activities.
- Listen. It is all too easy to let your mind wander to what's for supper or whether there are enough shirts ironed for tomorrow, and miss something significant or important in your child's blow-by-blow account of the day's activities.
- Tell her how you feel, and share some (but obviously not all) of your own concerns. She will learn from you the language and concepts she needs to describe her own feelings.

Part of listening to your child is accepting the way she says she feels. If you don't, she will not only feel frustrated and angry, but will eventually give up trying to tell you how she feels altogether. This may sound obvious, but how often have you heard the following exchanges?

4-year-old:	Mum, it's boring here. I want to go home.
Mum:	No, you don't.
8-year-old:	I hate my big brother, I wish he'd go and live somewhere else.
Dad:	Don't say things like that. You know you don't mean it.

12-year-old:	Mum, I don't want to go to that school any more – I don't like it.
Mum:	Nonsense, you've always loved it there!

It is much more helpful to the child if you can accept the way she feels at the moment, sympathize, and help her to explore her feelings further, and perhaps find a solution to the underlying problem.

Expecting the best

Children make easy scapegoats, and in some families children, or more often one child in particular, are never given the benefit of the doubt. Sometimes the whole family will tacitly elect just one of their number to take the blame for more or less everything that goes wrong. If one child is more accident-prone, or clumsy, or just younger than the others, there may well be some grounds for the suspicion that he is behind the broken plant pot, the lost football or the stained carpet, but we need to guard against jumping to this conclusion every time something goes wrong. Faced with low expectations, most children will live down to them – if everyone thinks the worst of you whatever you do, why bother to try? Getting the best out of your child means giving him every opportunity to do the right thing, respecting him enough to believe that he can and will do it most of the time, and telling him how pleased and proud you are when he does. If you can do this, he will live up to your expectations – most of the time.

In any transaction with your child, the aim should be to leave him feeling good about himself, even if he feels bad about something he has done, and believing in his own potential to do better next time.

The good enough parent

Perfect parenting is impossible, and parents can only do their best within their own limitations. We all find that we are more easily irritated at some times than others – tiredness, PMT and job or money worries can lower any parent's annoyance threshold considerably. If you know that you are under stress, and will not be able to avoid snapping at your child if she whines or misbehaves, it will make life a lot easier for her if you tell her so. Simply saying, 'Look, I'm feeling in a really bad mood/I've got a splitting headache, and it'd be best if you didn't annoy me right now,' is enough to give your child fair warning. Even if she persists, and you lose your temper, she will at least know that it isn't all her fault. It's OK for parents to make mistakes, as long as they don't pretend to be perfect, and apologizing to your child when you do sets the best example she could possibly have for handling her own mistakes.

A note on further reading

Family relationships and child-rearing are huge subjects in themselves. In this chapter I have illustrated some of the ways in which you can help to build your child's confidence in himself as he grows. I hope that these examples will inspire parents to learn more, and I have included a short reading list at the end of this book for those who want to carry their interest further. There are many more books available from your library or bookshop.

5

Health, Happiness and the Ability to Learn

It will be obvious to any parent that their child's physical and mental health will influence their ability to learn and develop, both at school and outside it. Poor nutrition, physical debility, tiredness and emotional upset reduce the ability to concentrate and to interpret information, and the immune system can be compromised, leading to frequent absences from school with minor or more serious illness. The child who is in good shape, both physically and mentally, will be able to make the most of the opportunities and challenges that school presents, and to enjoy life to the full both inside and outside school.

This common-sense conclusion has been backed up by numerous studies, and topics such as healthy eating, the importance of exercise and the dangers of drug and alcohol abuse are now part of the curriculum in both primary and secondary schools. Whatever they learn at school, however, the biggest influence on the health of school-age children is still what actually happens at home. A recent study concerning the health of school-age children found that 'Children, especially in primary school, seemed to have lively ongoing discussions with their parents about health matters, and to be proud of parents who were clearly living a healthy lifestyle.'

The same study found that teachers were concerned about the health of the children in their care, and the impact that this had on their ability to learn. These were their major concerns.

- Children didn't have enough sleep, and were tired during the day.
- Children had poor diets. They often missed breakfast, and school dinners were inadequate and not healthy enough.
- Children watched too much TV and missed out on traditional play which would benefit their talking, listening and responding skills.

- Children didn't get enough exercise, and had a poor level of physical fitness.
- Children (especially in secondary schools) were subject to high levels of stress and anxiety, often linked to frequent achievement testing.

These same issues have been raised by almost every teacher I have spoken to in the course of my research for this book, as having a major impact on children's ability to learn. Fortunately, these are areas where it is relatively easy for parents to make a difference, and a little forethought and planning will often pay dividends in terms of your child's fulfilment of his potential.

Sleep

Just by virtue of being a parent, you will understand only too well the importance of sleep. Do you remember your first few months with your new baby? Unless you were very lucky indeed, you spent at least a few weeks in a haze of broken nights and weary days. You had difficulty concentrating, forgot things, found normally easy tasks daunting and snapped at your partner over nothing, or burst into tears at the slightest provocation. Children need sleep just as much as adults do, and the child who is chronically short of sleep will be prey to health and behavioural problems and have difficulty facing the challenges of school life.

It is difficult to say how much sleep children need, and there is naturally some variation from child to child, but it is probably true to say that most primary schoolchildren should be in bed by 7.30–8 p.m. on a school night, and secondary schoolchildren by 9–10 p.m., depending on their age.

Reasonable bedtimes are relatively easy to achieve in the winter months, but as the evenings draw out in the late spring and summer it gets harder and harder for a child to get to sleep until dusk falls and the noises outside die away. There is nothing to be gained by forcing a wakeful child to stay in bed for hours on end, but whatever the time of year you can help your child to sleep by having a regular bedtime routine, by spending time with him, reading and talking in bed while he winds down, and by ensuring that he has plenty of exercise and mental stimulation during the day, and is actually tired at bedtime. If you are not sure whether your child is getting enough sleep, ask his teacher whether he seems tired at school.

Younger children sometimes get very tired at mid-morning or mid-afternoon when they first start school. Often this is because they are used to eating little and often at home, and they find the break between breakfast and lunch, or lunch and home-time, just too long for them to manage without a snack – they simply run out of energy. If you think that this is the case for your child, ask his teacher if he can bring a piece of fruit or some raisins to school to eat during break. Most children grow out of this phase quite quickly.

Nutrition

It is very important that children eat healthily right from the start. There are three reasons for this.

- Optimum growth and development requires good nutrition.
- A good diet will give your child the energy she needs to fill her days with constructive play and, later, work.
- Good dietary habits established in childhood will persist into adult life, and benefit long-term health.

Nutrition is a complex subject, and there is a great deal of information available concerning the basics of a healthy diet. If you observe the following rules, however, you won't go far wrong.

Food should be fun

Food can only provide nourishment if it is eaten. Making your child's meals varied, interesting and tasty, and making mealtimes a time to relax and be together with the family, will help him to establish good eating habits and take his diet seriously.

Provide a variety of foods

A balanced diet must include foods from each of the five main groups, in about the following proportions: fruit and vegetables 30 per cent, bread, cereals and potatoes 30 per cent, meat, fish, pulses, Quorn, etc. 15 per cent, dairy foods 15 per cent, fat and sugary foods 10 per cent. There is lots of variety to choose from within these groups, so healthy food need never be boring. It's all right to include some of those foods we think of as less healthy, such as chips and burgers, but these should never form the main part of a child's diet.

Watch your child's weight

Being overweight and underweight are both bad for long-term health. Most children will eat enough for their needs as long as a variety of healthy foods are available, and underweight in school-age children is quite rare and requires investigation. Obesity among children, sadly, is common and on the increase. It is likely that the reason for this is twofold:

- Consumption of large quantities of sweet and fatty foods (crisps, sweet drinks, chocolate and confectionery, etc.).
- Less exercise. Only 59 per cent of children now walk to school and 2 per cent cycle, while 81 per cent of journeys to school take only ten minutes or less to walk. Parents are less likely to allow children to 'play out' because of the risks from heavy traffic and the perceived risk from paedophiles, and television and computer games have become main sources of entertainment at home.

If your child is overweight, try to increase the amount of exercise he takes and to change the sort of foods he eats, cutting down on snacks and increasing fruit, vegetables and unrefined foods. *Never* put a child 'on a diet' unless your doctor advises it, as this could fail to supply all the nutrients he needs for healthy growth and development. It could also make food an 'issue' for him, possibly leading to eating disorders. If you are worried about your child's weight, or feel that he may be developing an eating disorder, ask your doctor for advice.

Breakfast

Studies have shown that eating breakfast improves children's problem-solving abilities, memory, concentration levels, visual perception and creative thinking. Teachers, too, are adamant that many children are unable to perform to their full potential at school because they do not eat a proper breakfast.

You can help your child by making sure that he gets up in time to eat a proper breakfast, ideally containing complex carbohydrates – wholemeal bread or cereals, for example – which break down more slowly in the body than refined foods and provide a more consistent release of energy into the bloodstream. Avoid sugared cereals and other very sweet things for breakfast, as they prompt a quick release of energy, followed by a correspondingly quick fall in blood sugar, which causes tiredness.

Some schools offer breakfast clubs, which open up to an hour before school starts, and provide a substantial breakfast for a small charge. Sometimes a period of learning activities takes place after the meal. Particularly helpful where both parents work, these clubs provide an excellent opportunity for children to develop their social skills and confidence while starting the day with a proper meal.

Lunch

One of the choices you will have to make when your child starts school is between packed lunches or the meals the school provides. The local education authority decides on the presentation, cost and content of school meals, and often buys in the whole service from an outside caterer. Sometimes the meals are cooked on the premises, but the meals for smaller schools may be cooked elsewhere and brought into the school in insulated containers. This restricts the amount of choice that can be offered to the children, as supplies of popular choices cannot be topped up and seconds may not be available. Most menus now allow for a vegetarian alternative to meat-based meals, but you should talk to the school if your child has special dietary requirements.

The school should be able to show you a sample menu, and you can talk to existing parents at the school about quality, size of portions, etc. Free school meals, and break-time milk where schools provide it, are available for children whose parents receive certain benefits and, in some circumstances, for the children of students. The LEA will be able to provide more information about free school meals and milk.

The choice between school meals and packed lunches is not entirely straightforward, and there are points both in favour of and against both options.

Packed lunches

In favour:

- You know what your child is eating.
- Packed meals can work out cheaper than school dinners.
- Special dietary requirements can be catered for (e.g. vegetarian, dairy allergy).
- Your child will not need to take money to school – a potential magnet for bullies.

Against:

- Few schools have refrigerated storage for packed lunches, which may stand in a hot classroom for hours before being consumed, with obvious health risks.
- Preparing several packed lunches during the morning rush to get everyone out of the house can be a real burden.
- Thinking of healthy lunch foods that will not deteriorate in the lunch box, and that children will actually eat, can be quite a challenge.
- Children sometimes 'share' their lunch boxes with friends, and your child may be eating less than you think.

School dinners

In favour:

- School dinners can provide a cooked meal at a relatively low price. For some children, this is their only cooked meal of the day.

- Sharing a cooked meal with others helps children to develop their social skills.
- Buying dinners, where the school operates a cafeteria-style system, can help children to learn about money and its worth.

Against:

- Portions can be very small. This can be a problem in smaller primary schools, where the child will usually get a set meal with no opportunity for seconds. Some children's energy requirements are not met by the standard portion size.
- Although healthy meals may be available, there is often nothing to stop children from choosing chips and a fizzy drink followed by chocolate mousse, for instance, for every meal, particularly at secondary schools.
- Carrying dinner money can attract bullies and thieves to your child.

Perhaps the best compromise, where the school allows it, is to provide your child with a packed lunch on some days, and send her to school with dinner money on days when you're rushed, or there is something that she particularly likes on the menu.

Exercise

We all know that exercise is good for us, but how much exercise should our children be getting? The Health Education Authority (HEA) makes the following recommendations.

- All young people should participate in one hour per day of moderate physical activity.
- Young people who currently do little activity should partici-pate in physical activity of at least moderate intensity for at least half an hour per day.
- At least twice a week, some of these activities should help to enhance and maintain muscular strength and flexibility and bone health.

This should be enough, according to the HEA, to:

- optimize physical fitness, current health, and growth and development;
- reduce the risk of chronic diseases later in life;
- develop active lifestyles at an early age to encourage the exercise habit.

Research has shown that many young people don't meet this target. Although most accumulate at least 30 minutes of moderate physical activity on most days of the week, made up of short bursts of activity rather than sustained effort, this is not considered enough to benefit their health. It is not necessary for children to take part in very strenuous activity in order to gain health benefits. Moderate levels of activity equivalent to brisk walking are quite sufficient to count towards the target of one hour a day. Walking to and from school, where it is possible and safe for a child to do so, can therefore fulfil part or all of your child's exercise requirement for the day.

Younger children, given the opportunity both in the school playground and at home, will take a good deal of exercise in the course of running around and 'letting off steam'. This declines as children mature, and it is particularly important that older children are encouraged to take part in physical activities, especially as they reach adolescence. Girls tend to decrease the amount of exercise they take even more than boys, who remain more active throughout childhood and adolescence.

The National Curriculum requires schools to promote physical activity and healthy lifestyles, and physical education lessons will fulfil a small part of your child's exercise requirement. Schools can also help by getting together with local sports clubs to encourage children to take part in sport regularly outside school. School activities weeks and summer activities often introduce children to sports they may choose to continue in their own time. It would not be realistic to expect school to make more than a small contribution to your child's overall exercise requirement, however, and you will probably need to encourage physical

activities outside school yourself in order to ensure that your
child meets his exercise requirement.

- Encourage your child to walk or cycle to and from school.
- Encourage your child to join local sports clubs.
- Take exercise as a family at weekends (walking, cycling,
  swimming, etc.).

Stress

Stress is a natural reaction to challenging circumstances, and the
physical changes it induces – increased adrenaline production
and heart rate, a rush of energy and so on – prepare us for 'fight
or flight'. In certain circumstances, for instance the start of a
sporting competition or a difficult interview, this can help us to
give of our best. When stress is prolonged, however, it can lead to
physical and emotional problems.

It is important that parents recognize the symptoms of stress in
their children, and act to relieve it when it occurs. Children who
are subjected to prolonged periods of stress can, just like adults,
lapse into depression or ill-health and lose the confidence and
motivation to take on the challenges of life. The following signs
can be indicators that your child is under more stress than she can
easily cope with.

- Physical tension – being 'like a coiled spring'.
- Difficulty sleeping.
- Increased susceptibility to minor infections – colds, sore
  throats, skin rashes, etc.
- Irritability.

It may be obvious what is causing your child's stress reaction –
exams, family arguments, etc. – but if it is not, try to talk to your
child about what is worrying her. Make an appointment to talk to
your child's teacher, too – he will be able to find out whether
there is a problem at school that your child hasn't mentioned.

Even if she doesn't want to talk about her current problem, you can help by talking generally about stress and how to handle it, and reassuring her that she is doing OK as far as you are concerned, and needn't face any problems alone.

As we get older, we all learn to cope with stress, to a greater or lesser extent. For the child facing stressful events for the first time, however, the temptation may be to avoid or escape from the stressful situation, or to pretend that it is not happening. This doesn't work as a long-term strategy, however, as it is impossible to master any new skills or face any challenges without experiencing some degree of stress. The key is to learn to face stress positively. Here are some suggestions that you can make to your stressed child.

- Remember that everyone gets stressed at times – there is nothing wrong with you.
- Confronting your stressful situation and doing your best will make you feel much better about yourself, even if you are not successful, than running away – and the situation will be far less stressful the next time.
- Learning self-relaxation techniques can help you to cope with stressful moments.
- Listing the reasons why you are well equipped to face this challenge can help you to view it more positively: 'I always get good marks in this subject,' 'I have trained hard for this competition,' 'I am good at sticking up for myself without losing my temper.'
- Even if things go badly, you still have a family that loves and admires you, and respects you for having a go.

Bullying, parents' relationship problems or marital breakdown, loneliness and feelings of inadequacy and many other common situations can cause children stress from which they cannot find relief without help. In these cases, parents must take a hand to tackle the cause of the stress directly, or find the help that the child needs from outside sources. Your doctor's surgery or library should be able to tell you about local sources of help and counselling for young people.

Depression

Depression is more than just feeling a bit low or unhappy – it is a serious condition that can prevent the sufferer from getting on with his life, and leave him feeling that there is no hope, and no point in carrying on.

Even very young children can and do become depressed, and it is important that parents are able to recognize the signs of depression, which can include some (but not usually all) of the following.

- A general feeling of misery.
- Moodiness – often there is a pattern with the sufferer feeling worse in the morning and better as the day goes on, but this may be reversed.
- Disturbed sleep.
- Anxiety.
- Irritability.
- Lack of energy.
- Thinking, speaking and moving more slowly than usual.
- Difficulty concentrating.
- Forgetfulness.
- Inability to enjoy things that are normally fun.
- Worries about the future – hopelessness.
- Low self-esteem and guilt.
- Hypochondria.
- Loss of appetite.

Of course, depression is not 'caught' like a cold – there is usually a progression from simply feeling a bit low to full-blown depressive illness. If you think that your child is sliding towards depression, it is important to tackle the problem before it becomes more serious. Talk to your GP, who will be able to suggest sources of counselling or other help.

6

Practical Ways to Help

It's all too easy to continue to do everyday things for our children long after they are capable of doing them for themselves. By the time your child starts school, however, he should have learned and practised the following basic skills.

- Using the toilet properly, and flushing it after use. If your child is a boy, make sure that he knows how to use a urinal – he may otherwise embarrass himself by pulling his trousers down.
- Getting his coat on and off by himself, and hanging it on a peg.
- Washing and drying his hands.
- Dressing and undressing himself.
- Using a tissue to blow his nose.
- Putting on his shoes. This will be easier if you buy shoes that fasten with velcro or buckles.
- Using a knife and fork.
- Sharing and taking turns with others.

Knowing that he doesn't have to rely on you for these essentials will help give your child the confidence to be away from you, and his teacher will bless you for your foresight!

Getting to school

Entitlement to school transport

If your child is attending the nearest suitable school for your area and it is more than 2 miles away by the shortest walking route for children under 8, or 3 miles for pupils between 8 and 16, you are entitled to free school transport. Lesser distances are held to be walkable, although there are very few parents who would expect or allow their 8-year-old to undertake a 3-mile walk to and from school each day.

Even if your child does not attend the nearest suitable school, the LEA may sometimes agree to pay all or part of her travelling expenses, or allow her to use a spare seat on the school bus. Children who have received a statement of special educational needs, whose assessment found that they needed transport to school, will also receive free transport. Children who attend a particular school on religious grounds and some over-16s may also be entitled to help.

If you think that your child should receive free school transport, you should ask your LEA for details and application forms.

Taking the car

If you have a car, you can of course drive your child to school. There are several arguments against this.

- Walking or cycling to school is healthier for your child.
- The sheer volume of school-going traffic (20 per cent of the total at peak times) is causing major problems on our roads, particularly in our cities.
- The pollution that car use causes is having a major impact on the world our children will inherit.
- Children who become dependent on the car will be less likely to take up the healthy alternatives of walking or cycling later in life.

Many school journeys are for less than a mile, and it is worth considering carefully the alternatives to getting the car out to make such a short journey. If you have to take the car to school, consider sharing the trip with other parents, saving yourself time and petrol and saving your community traffic congestion and air pollution.

Alternatives to the car

Public transport

In some areas there may be public transport that will get your child to, or near to school. Train and bus companies often run special discount schemes for students and young people, so it is worth checking with your local company for any reductions that may be available.

Walking with your child

Walking your child to school will give him the opportunity to learn road safety and traffic awareness, skills that will stand him in good stead when he starts to become independent. Your child will become used to taking a little exercise each day – a healthy habit to establish early in life – his fitness will improve, and he will start his school day alert and fresh into the bargain.

The walking bus

In some areas, primary schools have instituted a 'walking bus' scheme. Children walk together to school, supervised by adults (often parent volunteers) and calling at prearranged 'stops' to collect 'passengers'. This nicely overcomes parents' fears over allowing young children to walk to school unsupervised, and means that no one parent need commit an hour or more at each end of every day in order to get the benefits of walking to school for their child.

Cycling

For the older child, cycling is an excellent means of getting to school, but make sure that your child has undertaken cycling proficiency training first. Primary schools often offer cycling proficiency courses to their pupils, usually run by parents who have had special training from their LEA. If your school doesn't offer training, you could suggest it to your head teacher, and volunteer to run or help with the course.

School uniform and personal appearance

There is no national policy on school uniform, and it is up to school governors to decide whether their school should have a uniform or dress code and, if so, what it should be. Head teachers will decide how any school rules regarding uniform will be enforced. Where there is a school uniform, LEAs can offer grants towards its cost to families who qualify. Contact your LEA for details if you are receiving benefits or on a low income.

Many primary schools have quite relaxed uniform requirements or none at all, while secondary schools tend to have much stricter rules regarding clothing. Unfortunately, while primary-age children are usually quite unconcerned about what they wear to school, secondary-age children often hate their school uniform with a passion, and will do anything to get around its restrictions, to the point of open rebellion. There are, however, certain advantages to the wearing of school uniform:

- Less opportunity for bullying and teasing on the grounds of appearance.
- A common appearance can help children to feel a part of the school community.
- Children can more easily be identified on out-of-school trips.
- No dispute at home about what is and is not suitable for school wear.
- The school can raise a little much-needed revenue on the sale of uniform items.

While there are many good reasons for schools insisting on a uniform there are also some disadvantages:

- Uniform can discriminate against some groups, i.e. girls may not be allowed to wear trousers.
- Uniform items are often available only from one supplier, and can be expensive.
- The items chosen for school uniform are sometimes impractically difficult to care for.
- School uniform can be unpopular with those who have to wear it.

Cutting the cost

Many schools hold a school uniform sale at the beginning of the school year, at which both second-hand and new uniform items will be available. This can lessen the impact of buying a complete uniform in one go when your child starts at a new school. If your school doesn't do this already, why not suggest to the PTA that it starts a uniform exchange? The clothing stall at the school fair can also be a good source of second-hand uniform items.

If your child's school uniform is impractical, unduly expensive or discriminatory, you can approach the governing body with suggestions for change. Be warned that this can be very hard going, as some school governors will guard fiercely the traditions of the school they have been associated with for many years, but if you are polite but persistent and have the support of other parents they will probably listen to you eventually.

While school uniform or dress code are usually covered by a written policy, matters of personal appearance such as hairstyle and body-piercing are rarely covered in detail. Occasionally the whole issue of personal appearance becomes a battleground, often between parents and school with the child stuck somewhere in the middle, and there have been a few well-publicized cases of head teachers suspending children because of what they consider unsuitable haircuts.

Common sense usually prevails in the end. Where a hairstyle does not look unduly unkempt, or impair a child's ability to learn, it would be hard for a head teacher to justify depriving a child of his education on the grounds of taste alone – but it is regrettable that the child's education has been interrupted and his relationship with the school has been soured. If your child is considering a change of style, it is worth anticipating any problems that may arise, and avoiding confrontation as far as possible, even if you think that the rules are somewhat arbitrary. If your child wants to look different, try the following suggestions.

- Dye hair unusual colours over the summer holidays, with semi-permanent dye that will wash out before school goes back.
- For pierced ears, nose, etc., use discreet hoops or studs at school, and be prepared to tape them over for PE.
- Choose a haircut that can be rendered fairly normal-looking for school, either by tying up or gelling down.

- Use temporary, transfer-type tattoos or body-paint, and wash them off for school.

Issues of personal liberty can arouse very strong feelings in both children and parents, but it is worth remembering that very few of us are free to look or behave exactly as we wish all the time. Whether it is wearing uniform for school or designer-distressed jeans for a party, we are all conforming to the requirements of one group or another.

Reading

One of the key areas in which you can help your child to progress at school is in learning to read. Reading fluently requires constant practice, and it is just not possible for teachers to provide the hours of one-to-one help that children need. Long before your child starts school, you can begin to prepare her for reading.

- Look at picture books with your child. Show her how to handle a book, hold it the right way up and turn its pages.
- Talk to her about the contents of the book. Show her that the pictures relate to a story.
- Follow the words with your finger as you read them to your child. She will learn that written words on the page relate to spoken words.
- Read poetry to your child, as well as prose. Young children love the rhythms of poems and nursery rhymes, and develop a feeling for the meaning and use of words that is hard to convey in storybooks.
- Your child may surprise you by learning to recognize a few words before she starts school, but this is not the aim at this early stage. Simply learning to enjoy, value and care for books is a vital first step to reading.

Once your child has started school, she will bring home reading books to read with you. You will probably be asked to fill in a reading record, so that her teacher can see where your child has got to, and there will usually be space for your comments, so that you can note down any words she had difficulty with, anything she particularly liked about the story, and say how you think she is progressing.

- Sit down with your child in a quiet, comfortable place with good light.
- Place the book on a firm surface so that it doesn't wobble about.
- Use a strip of card to cover the lines below that which she is reading or, later, encourage her to follow the words with her finger.
- Don't try to do too much at a time – a young child's concentration span is fairly short, and reading is hard work for beginners. Reading should always be enjoyable, and if a bit of encouragement doesn't make it so, stop and try again another time.
- Encourage your child to talk about the story, guess what might happen next, etc.
- Don't worry if your child's reading book sometimes seems too easy for her. Children tend to learn in spurts, with a period of consolidation in between, and reading a book that is well within her capabilities will give her confidence to improve further.
- Don't just stick to school reading books. Read with your child often from her own books, library books, children's magazines, cereal packets, street signs – anything at all that grabs her interest.

Older children still need encouragement to read, even after they have passed the stage of needing help with the reading itself and can tackle a whole book on their own. Children who read a lot increase their general knowledge and become proficient at finding the information they need to complete their homework and projects, and rarely have trouble with spelling.

- Read some of your child's books yourself, and talk with her about what makes them good, bad or indifferent.
- Encourage her to join your local library and take part in any reading schemes they offer.

- Give, and ask others to give, book tokens for birthday and Christmas presents. Make a big outing of a trip to the bookshop to spend the tokens.
- Encourage your child to read about hobbies and sports she is interested in. Magazines are just as good as books for reading practice, and can be very informative.

Learning resources

Libraries

Libraries are a wonderful source of information and entertainment, and are now much more child-friendly than they were a generation ago. As well as fiction, non-fiction and reference books, most libraries now lend videos, music CDs and DVDs and offer public access computers. If you have one within reach, it is well worth making visits to the library a regular part of your child's life from the time he first starts to enjoy books. By the time he needs to use the library's resources for help with his school work he will feel at home there and know where and how to look for the information he needs.

Reference books

A good set of encyclopaedias used to be the ultimate homework reference tool, and many families made great sacrifices to buy this expensive advantage for their children. Since the advent of personal computers, however, it has become possible for parents to provide their child with a complete encyclopaedia on CD or DVD for a tiny fraction of the price of the good printed version. Using reference books, however, is still a useful skill, and a great deal of information is still not available, or is hard to find, on disc or over the Internet.

Most families have a few reference books on common subjects – dictionary, thesaurus, wildlife guide, gardening manual, etc. – and there are many more available, both to buy and from the library. You can encourage your child to use these whenever he expresses an interest or asks a question.

Computers

Your child will have access to computers at school, and will learn to use them in IT (information technology) lessons. There are, however, a number of advantages to be gained from having a computer at home.

- The preparation and presentation of projects will be easier and more effective.
- He will not have to compete for the limited time available on school computers.
- Familiarity with the PC will be required in further education and for many jobs.
- Much of the research that your child needs to do for his school work can most easily be done over the Internet.

If you decide to buy a computer but don't have any knowledge or experience in the field, the choice can be bewildering. Before you buy, invest in one or two of the many computer magazines available, and find out which manufacturer they recommend. This is a complicated and constantly changing issue, but there are some basic buying tips that hold good, whatever the latest chips, drives or gimmicks.

- Buy the best-specified machine (in terms of processor speed, memory and disk space) that you can afford. Poorly specified machines can be amazingly cheap, but this is because new software will not run properly on them.
- Get the best manufacturer's warranty that you can.
- Make sure that your machine is protected against viruses. Some come with a virus checker, but budget for buying one if yours does not.

Safe use of the Internet

The Internet gives access to an enormous amount of useful and stimulating material for children, but it is not without its problems. The main dangers of allowing children unrestricted Internet access are:

- They may encounter pornographic, violent or otherwise unsuitable or upsetting material.
- They may meet paedophiles or other dangerous individuals through their use of chat rooms.
- They may waste considerable amounts of time and money browsing through the vast amount of pointless and trivial material that exists alongside the worthwhile content.

There are several ways in which you can monitor and control your child's use of the Internet.

- *Keep an eye on things*. Site the computer somewhere you can see it – a family room rather than a child's bedroom, for example. You can then check occasionally on the sites your child is accessing, and he will be less tempted to look for material that you would rather he didn't see.
- *Set up family rules*. Once you have explained to your children the dangers of using the Internet you can, as a family, agree rules covering its use. This could include such things as the times at which the Internet can be accessed, what it can be used for and who can use it, as well as a family policy concerning the use by older children of sites with violent or sexual content when younger children are around.
- *Use software that filters out adult content*. Many internet service providers (ISPs) offer free software that aims to filter out sites containing material unsuitable for children, or it can be purchased independently of your ISP. This software is not infallible, however, and some supervision is still essential.

If a young child accidentally comes across text or images which are unpleasant or disturbing, it is important to reassure him that it is not his fault.

Help with language problems

Children whose language skills are below average are obviously at a disadvantage at school, so helping your child to appreciate the possibilities of the spoken word from the very start, by talking to and with her about her surroundings, her feelings and her experiences, is an important way of helping her to get the most from school.

This is more difficult in families for whom English is an additional language, and one in which the adults may find it difficult to express themselves spontaneously and clearly. If this is the case in your family, your child may need extra help when she starts at a school where English is the language used for teaching.

If you think that your child may find it difficult at school because English is not her first language, ask the primary schools you are considering specifically about this point before you make a decision. Local authorities with large numbers of EAL (English as an additional language) children in their schools will have developed strategies and teaching materials to help meet the additional needs of these children, but in areas where there is a small ethnic minority population there may be no system in place to cater for their needs.

If your child is already having problems with language, don't delay in talking to her teacher about it, and asking for extra help. (Information on resources for schools, as well as recommendations for parents on ways to help children with literacy, is available from the National Literacy Trust web site – see Useful Addresses). You could also approach your LEA and ask whether they can provide assistance or information.

Exams and tests

Most exams now depend, at least in part, on an assessment of coursework, so the awful pressure of having your whole future depend on what you can get down on paper in a couple of hours has eased somewhat. Taking exams is still taxing and stressful, however, and it starts a good deal younger than it used to. Key Stage Tests have introduced children as young as 7 to the pressure of examinations, and many teachers and parents feel that children can and sometimes do suffer anxiety and distress as a result. See Chapter 5 for the warning signs and how to deal with them.

Helping your primary-age child cope with tests

Your child's teachers should be aware of the danger of stressing your child by placing undue importance on 'success' or 'failure' in tests, and do everything possible to minimize the pressure he is put under. However, since the results of the tests are made public and directly affect perception of the competence of the candidates' teachers, they would be less than human if they didn't badly want to achieve the best possible result. This cannot fail to communicate itself to the children, however hard teachers try to lessen the impact, and some children will become anxious about the tests as a result.

In some schools there is little attempt to minimize this danger, and there are many stories circulating in teaching circles about PE lessons cancelled in favour of cramming for tests, threats and bribery directed at children and teachers falsifying results. These are probably not common events, but it does give us an indication of the pressure that teachers feel they are under, and which must communicate itself to at least some children.

You can help your child by explaining to him that the tests have no real significance for him – how he does will not affect his future or what he does at school. Tell him that, although it is always a good idea to do your best in whatever task you undertake, he doesn't need to worry in this instance that his best will not be good enough. The tests are designed to find out how well his teachers have taught him, not how hard he has worked. Try to help him see the tests as an interesting challenge rather than a grim responsibility.

If you feel strongly that your child is being put under undue pressure, you are at liberty to withdraw him from the tests.

Helping your secondary-age child cope with tests and exams

At secondary school, the pressure of tests and exams really kicks in. With GCSEs on the horizon and the choice of options imminent, even the school's internal tests can seem crucial. It is difficult, as a parent, to find a balance between impressing on your child the importance of doing her best, and helping her to keep things in proportion. The following tips may help.

- Listen to and acknowledge the way your child tells you she is feeling, even if you would rather that she didn't feel that way. Understand that she may find it easier to talk to someone else – maybe a friend or teacher – about her worries.
- Make allowances for the stress she's under. If she becomes moody, withdrawn or irritable, try to understand that it's because she's feeling the strain, and reassure rather than reject her.
- Don't make it worse. Most children are well aware that their exams are important – that's why they're stressed. Constantly reminding them how devastatingly awful it would be for them to fail will just make matters worse.
- Let her find her own way of organizing herself. Imposing a timetable on her is unlikely to work, so encourage her to find a study routine that she can live with – if this means staying up half the night and sleeping late in the day, so be it.
- Don't threaten – few things are more demotivating than the threat of retribution if you fail. Your child needs to know that you will continue to accept and love her whatever her results, and that the approval of her parents doesn't depend on her success or failure.
- Encourage your child (and try yourself) to have realistic expectations of what she can achieve. If she is to use her time to best effect, she needs to gauge her strengths and weaknesses accurately, and plan to use her efforts where they will gain the most benefits.
- Be aware of the warning signs that stress is building up to overwhelming levels (see Chapter 5) and be prepared to step in if they do.

It will help if both you and your child can see exams an exciting challenge to be tackled, and an opportunity to do well, rather than as a depressing opportunity for failure. Don't forget that, however important it seems at the time, passing examinations is not the most important thing in life, and failing them is not the end of everything. If the worst comes to the worst, and your child doesn't pass the exams she needs in order to do what she really wants, there are ways round it. Exams can be retaken, either straightaway or later on in life when she knows what she wants and is motivated to achieve it. Exams are not an end in themselves, but one way to doing what you want to do with your life.

Relaxation

Part of helping our children to do well academically is making sure that they don't work too hard. We are all familiar with the old adage, 'All work and no play makes Jack a dull boy', and in this context dull doesn't just mean boring. It means blunt, jaded, lacking in enthusiasm and energy, and unable to give of one's best when faced with a challenge.

Some children will react to a daunting workload by giving up, while others will throw themselves into desperate overwork in an attempt to gain control of the situation. Both these children will benefit from an organized and fairly structured approach to their work with achievable short-term goals and planned breaks for relaxation.

Equipment

At primary school, everything your child needs to use during the school day will usually be provided by the school. Sometimes, however, children prefer to take their own pen, colouring pencils, calculator and so on, as those provided by the school may have to be shared. Often pupils will not be allowed to take home the school's equipment, so they will need their own for homework.

In secondary school, pupils are usually expected to provide their own equipment. Schools will send out a list to new pupils before they start, and it is important that you provide your child with all the equipment on the list, and replace it as necessary. Secondary pupils do not normally have a desk or drawer at school in which to leave their books and equipment, and have to take everything they need for the day in their school bag. Some schools have lockers for pupils' use, and often a deposit will be required for the key. This can provide a useful place to stow books that are not needed immediately, and lightens the load that must be carried around school all day.

There is concern about the effect on children's backs of carrying heavy bags to, from and around school all day. To avoid back trouble, ensure that your child:

- has a well-designed, backpack type bag;
- carries it squarely on her back, not in one hand;
- knows the correct way to lift heavy objects – bending the knees rather than the back, and holding the weight close to the body.

What teachers want

The most common plea from primary teachers was: 'Please, ask parents to check their child's book bag every day', followed by, 'Don't send in precious objects to show and tell'. For secondary teachers, sending children to school with a full set of equipment – pens, colouring pencils, etc. – was a priority. Sometimes the few children who do have everything needed for a particular task (usually girls, I'm told) end up sharing it with half the class.

The least we can do in support of our children's education is to present them at the school gates on time, well fed, well rested, properly dressed and fully equipped. These simple measures alone can make a world of difference to their school experience, and potentially affect their levels of achievement throughout their school career.

7

Homework

From the start, your child will be expected to complete some tasks related to his school work at home. The government guidelines on homework give a broad indication of how much time pupils of different ages might reasonably be expected to spend on homework.

Primary school:
Years 1, 2 and 3	1 hour per week
Years 5 and 6	2 hours per week

Secondary school:
Years 7 and 8	45–90 minutes per day
Year 9	1–2 hours per day
Years 10 and 11	1–2 hours per day

These figures represent a maximum, and the guidelines emphasize that it is more important that the homework is suitable for your child and contributes to his learning than that it fills a certain amount of time.

What is homework?

Homework will not always involve writing essays or answering questions, and may often not be written work at all. For young children it might involve simply reading together or playing games. Older children may be asked to gather information on a specific subject, practise spelling or tables, read, cook, try a simple experiment, find or make something. These are things that it might be difficult to do at school, and therefore they make an important contribution to your child's education that cannot be made in the school setting. Often, your input is vital, although there will be times when your child's teachers want to see how he can get on with the task alone.

How can you help?

First, by just being interested. Studies have shown that children do better at school when their parents take an interest in their work, and simply recognizing your child's efforts and providing encouragement will go a long way towards motivating and rewarding her.

You can also help in more practical ways, by answering your child's questions and providing her with facilities and resources that will help her with her work. You do need to beware, however, of the temptation to take over and do her homework for her. She needs to be able to work independently, and to develop confidence in her own ability to complete the tasks her teachers set her.

DO:

- *Make sure she has somewhere to work.* She will need a surface on which to work and a chair in a comfortable room with plenty of light.
- *Ensure she has peace and quiet.* Although homework is best done away from distractions like the TV, most children prefer to have some company, or even a radio playing in the background. Sometimes the kitchen table, with a parent present and available for help if asked, is better than isolation in a bedroom, however good the facilities.
- *Provide basic equipment.* Pens, pencils, crayons, ruler, paper and reference material such as an encyclopaedia. If you have a computer and printer, this can be used to produce work and, if you also have a modem, to access the Internet for information.
- *Establish a regular homework time.* Early evening, after your child has changed and eaten, but before she is too tired, is a good time for homework.
- *Allow her to work with friends.* She will probably appreciate

84

having a friend around to work with occasionally, and in projects where children are collaborating, this may be essential.

- *Make sure that finished homework is handed in.* Once finished, homework should be stored safely away from toddlers, pets and spills. If it can be handed in straightaway, it should go back into the school bag ready for school the next day. Have a shelf, cupboard or folder set aside for finished homework, and remind your child to check it every morning for items that should be handed in that day.

- *Above all, remember that homework can be fun.* Finding out can be an exciting business, and trips to museums, libraries and all sorts of other places to gather information can involve the whole family. Sometimes research for homework can spark off new interests and activities for your child and yourself.

DON'T:

- *Take over.* Provide the means to find the information he needs, and help in finding it if necessary, but allow your child to draw his own conclusions and write up the result in his own words – in discussion with you if need be.

- *Pretend you know everything.* Allow your child to tell you about what he has learned, and ask him to explain things you don't understand. He will consolidate his knowledge in explaining it to you, and his confidence will get an enormous boost.

- *Be too rigid about when homework is done.* Your child needs to take part in other activities outside school and to see his friends sometimes. Very little homework is due in the day after it is set, and missing a homework session from time to time will not matter overly – your child can simply catch up the next day.

- *Assume it is your child's fault if he is struggling with his homework.* All homework activities should be related to work children are doing at school, and schools and teachers are expected to organize homework carefully so that children are not expected to do too much on any one day. If he can't cope, let the school know.

Homework clubs

For hard-pressed working parents, and those with several young children or living in cramped accommodation, it can be almost impossible to find the time to help children with homework, or the space and facilities to allow them to do it properly. Some schools already provide a supervised place to do homework, after or during school, and funding has been made available by the government to increase this sort of provision, either within schools or in other places such as libraries or halls. Children themselves may often appreciate the chance to do their homework with their friends, and find it easier to concentrate in a setting with less distractions than home.

Homework diaries

Many secondary schools provide their pupils with a homework diary – sometimes this is incorporated in the more general record book. The child uses the diary to record homework she is given and when it has to be handed in, and many schools require teachers and/or parents to sign the diary on a weekly, or even daily, basis. This shows that everyone is being kept informed about what the child is supposed to be doing, and what she actually does.

There is usually a space for parents to write comments in the homework diary, and you can use this space to let the school know if:

- your child found homework too hard or too easy;
- your child was unable to do the homework for some reason (lost book, etc.);
- homework has not been marked;
- no homework has been set.

Feedback

Few things are more demotivating for a child than to put a great deal of effort into a piece of work, only to find that it is still unmarked weeks later, or that the teacher has only skimmed through it, or given it an almost arbitrary mark. Teachers are often very hard-pressed, but this is an important issue and they have certain expectations to live up to. They must give children feedback on their homework, letting them know how well they have done, and how they could do better. This can be done through discussion in lessons, or through written comments on their work.

If several pieces of homework in the same subject remain unmarked, or it appears that a teacher has overlooked serious mistakes in your child's work, or not given sufficient acknowledgement of his efforts, you should contact the school (see Chapter 2).

Homework policy

Every school should have a written homework policy, and must show it to you if you ask to see it. The DfES requires homework policies to state:

- when the school expects to review the policy;
- how parents will be involved in the review.

Homework does not exist to keep children busy after school, or simply to fulfil the DfES's requirements that homework be set, but should contribute to the children's progress. If it does not do this for your child, you should make this clear to the school.

8

When Things Go Wrong

However good the school you have chosen for your child, however happy he is there and however conscientiously you strive to prepare and support him, at some time during his school career something will go wrong. No school is completely without problems, and the real test of a good school is in how it recognizes and handles problems when they occur. Any school that denies having problems at all should be avoided: the school that claims to be completely bully-free cannot deal adequately with the bullying it undoubtedly contains. The school that is so confident in the way it has done things for years that it never reassesses its policies cannot respond to the ever-changing society within which it must operate.

Rights and obligations

Both parents and schools are bound by some obligations regarding their children, or the children in their care.

Parents' obligations

Parents and carers are responsible in law for making sure that their children are educated between the ages of 5 and 16.

- If your child is registered at a school (this excludes home-educated children), he or she must go to school on time every day during term-time, unless there is a good reason (such as illness). If they do not go to school regularly, you can be fined.
- Parents are responsible for telling the school if their child will be absent, and why.
- If attendance problems do develop, parents are expected to help the school and the education welfare service to solve the problems.

- Parents do not have a right to take children on holiday in term-time. The school must agree this beforehand, or the absence will be regarded as unauthorized.
- If your child is persistently absent without a good reason, the LEA can take legal action against you.

Schools' obligations

The statutory requirements placed on schools are enormously complex and constantly changing. Many of them relate to quite minor aspects of school life, and are unlikely to be of real interest to parents. If you feel that the school is falling down in what seems to be a key area of the education or care of your child, and your approaches to the school have not brought about a solution to the problem, it would be wise to contact the DfES and ask for information on legislation covering the area that is causing you concern. If the school is failing in a statutory duty, you will be fully justified in taking the matter to the LEA and, ultimately, the Secretary of State.

Home–school agreements

Every state school is required to produce its own home–school agreement, in consultation with its parents and pupils. The agreement is intended to explain the aims and values of the school, and to describe the responsibilities of school, pupils and parents. Parents and children will be asked to sign a copy of this agreement, to show that they understand and accept what is required of them in their relationship with the school.

Home school agreements have no standing in law – signing one does not legally bind you to fulfil the requirements that it lays down for parents or pupils, and no one can take legal action against you if you don't. Neither can your child be disciplined or excluded just for breaking the home–school agreement, unless this involves a serious breach of school discipline that would normally result in these measures. It is important, nevertheless, that you and your child read the agreement carefully before deciding whether to sign it, for the following reasons.

- It is an important principle to convey to your child that she should never sign any sort of contract or agreement without fully understanding and agreeing with the contents.
- The home–school agreement must be produced in consultation with parents and pupils at the school, and if you disagree with anything that is in it, it is your right to register your disagreement and suggest that it be revised. It is *not* a list of rules imposed by the school on its pupils and their parents.

Many home–school agreements contain a long list of very specific demands on the pupil and parent. For instance, they may require parents to: 'ensure that my child always wears the complete school uniform . . . arrives at school between 8.45 and 8.55, completes all his/her homework on time', and that children 'always obey the instructions of staff and classroom helpers promptly and without arguing'. The commitment of the school can be much less specific: '. . . will endeavour to provide a broad and balanced education based on the National Curriculum', for instance. If you disagree with a part of the agreement but are happy with the rest, you can cross out the part you disagree with before signing, or you are quite at liberty to refuse to sign it at all, like this parent:

> I was not against the idea of a home–school agreement. I felt that it was a good idea for the children to be consulted about the sort of rules of behaviour they thought were fair, and then to agree formally to keep them. I was especially concerned about bullying, and it seemed like a good chance for a school-wide discussion of what bullying really was, and that it was just not acceptable. When my children brought home the agreement, however, I was horrified. There was a vague reference to pupils treating each other with respect, but most of the pupils' part of the agreement said things like, 'I agree to always do my best', and 'I will always do what teachers tell me to do', or words to that effect. I can't honestly say that I *always* do my best, and I don't think that the staff at school could either, and I didn't think it was right that my children , in effect, should make a promise they couldn't keep. I was

particularly concerned about the undertaking always to do as they were told. I don't believe that anyone should *always* do as they are told without question. I returned the agreement to school unsigned and explained my reasons why, and no more was said about it.

The school cannot legally refuse entry to a child on the basis of non-signature of the home–school agreement.

What will the agreement contain?

There are certain basic issues that all home–school agreements will cover.

- *The standard of education the school will provide*
  This section will usually outline the statutory obligations of the school with regard to the education it provides for its pupils.
- *The 'ethos' of the school*
  This section may outline the general way that pupils are expected to behave, how they and the staff should treat each other and how the school relates to the wider community.
- *Attendance*
  The expectations of the school regarding attendance will be listed here – usually that your child goes to school regularly and turns up on time.
- *Discipline and behaviour*
  Pupils will be expected to keep to the school's rules, and you will be asked to agree to support the school in maintaining discipline.
- *Homework*
  Parents will be asked to agree to support the school's homework policy (which will be available from the school if you haven't seen it), and children will be asked to complete homework on time.
- *Communication between home and school*
  The school will normally undertake to keep you informed about your child's progress by means of written reports and parents' evenings, and ask you to tell them about any issues that might affect your child's work or behaviour.

Governing bodies can add to this basic agreement any issues that they feel are relevant to their individual school, and are bound by law to consult all their registered parents before introducing or amending a home–school agreement. The method they use to consult parents is left up to the school, and you are quite entitled to ask how your school consults its parents and whether there are any plans to change the current agreement. If you have strong feelings about the existing agreement, you should communicate them to the governing body. Schools are expected (although not obliged) to review home–school agreements every two or three years, and to consult parents as part of this procedure.

What if the school breaks the agreement?

Although the home–school agreement itself has no legal standing, schools will rarely undertake in an agreement to do more than they are statutorily obliged to do. If you feel that your school is not living up to the terms of its agreement you should approach the head teacher or the governing body with your concerns, regardless of whether you or your child have signed the agreement or kept to its terms.

Making your worries known

If you feel that things have gone wrong at school for your child, or for other children within your school community, how should you go about making your worries known? What action can you expect the school to take? Many schools will have a written policy describing their procedure for dealing with complaints from parents.

It is not helpful to characterize parents who are expressing concerns over their children's education or the school environment as 'complainers' – the school needs feedback from parents if it is to recognize and adapt to the needs of its pupils. Unfortunately, however, there is a 'them and us' culture in many schools that makes parents 'the enemy', and a parent who questions any aspect of the running of the school may be viewed with some hostility. 'Fussy mum', 'overprotective parent' and 'parent from hell' are phrases that crop up quite frequently between teachers in relation to parents who contact the school about issues that concern them, and teachers often feel that they are being accused of not doing their job properly, or of being less than professional, when parents comment unfavourably on things that happen at school.

If you do need to contact the school with a concern, therefore, do be aware that you are dealing with normal people who might, however professional they may be, find it quite difficult to deal with criticism. Your aim is to get your point listened to and action taken to remedy the problem, and inciting a defensive response will mitigate against any constructive outcome. However anxious, or even angry, you feel, try to take a calm and reasonable approach to the problem. If you feel that you won't be able to keep your cool in a face-to-face discussion, take your time and write a letter that states clearly all the points you want to make, then make an appointment to discuss them once the letter has been read. This will give both you and the recipient a chance to get over your initial aggressive and defensive reactions before you get together, and a constructive and useful discussion will be easier to achieve.

Don't wait

If you are worried about some aspect of your child's school experience, it is important that you talk to your child's teacher or the head teacher as soon as you can. If problems are caught early they can usually be sorted out informally and quickly, and prevented from escalating into more serious, long-term problems. This is particularly true of bullying, which should always be reported to your child's teacher straightaway.

Who should you approach, and how?

Your school is required by law to have a formal complaints procedure, and should be able to give you details of this. Normally, it will involve the following stages, with the complaint only moving on to the next stage if it has not been handled to everyone's satisfaction.

1 *Class teacher (primary) or form tutor (secondary)*
Your first approach to your child's class teacher or form tutor can be quite informal – a quick word after school or a telephone call – and this will often be enough to alert the school to what is going on and clear up any minor problems. Your secondary-age child's form tutor may pass you on to a subject teacher if your query is specific to that subject.

   If this initial approach doesn't get results, it is as well to follow it up with a note, reiterating what you said earlier and adding any new information. It is advisable to keep a note of what you have said, who you said it to and the date on which you said it, for future reference.

2 *Head of year (secondary only)*
And:

3 *Head teacher (primary and secondary) or deputy head (secondary)*
If you have to move on to the next stages, and talk to your secondary-age child's year head or your primary or secondary schoolchild's head teacher or deputy head (perhaps because your complaint is about your child's class teacher or form tutor) it is as well to make an appointment to talk to them, but also to note down the gist of your concern and either send it in beforehand, or take it in with you. Make two copies, one for the person you are meeting and one for you to refer to yourself during the discussion. Again, make notes of what was said and the date of your meeting. If any action is proposed, make a note of it and check that it has been taken within the time-frame agreed at your meeting.

4 *Board of governors (primary and secondary)*
Although parent governors are on the governing body to represent parents as a whole, and not officially to represent the views of individual parents, in practice they are often the only members of the governing body (apart from staff members) that parents see regularly. If you do need to approach the governors with a complaint that you feel has not been handled satisfactorily by the head teacher, a parent governor will probably be able to tell you how best and when to communicate your concern. School governors are best approached in

writing. List all the contact you have had with the school over this issue, any agreements that were made and any action taken, or agreed but not taken.

5 *LEA (primary and secondary)*
If your other approaches have failed, you can ask the LEA to look at your case. Your school complaints procedure or your governing body should tell you who to contact, but if this information is not available you can telephone the LEA and ask who your complaint should be directed to. You should send as detailed an account as possible of the problem you are complaining about, and of your dealings with the school and the governing body over this issue.

6 *The Secretary of State for Education (primary and secondary)*
In the last resort, if you feel that a governing body or LEA has failed to carry out a statutory duty or acted unreasonably, you can complain to the Secretary of State. If you wish to do this you should ask the DfES for advice on how to proceed.

Whenever you make a written approach to a staff member, the governors or the LEA, it is wise to follow your letter up, after a week or so, with a telephone call checking that it has arrived. Not only does this reassure you that your letter has not been lost in the post, but it also keeps it in the forefront of the recipient's mind, and ensures that it doesn't get lost under a pile of papers.

Whoever you approach, and however you approach them, remember:

- Be polite.
- Be reasonable.
- Be clear.
- Be concise.
- Keep a record of all contacts and decisions.

The DfES expects governing bodies and local education authorities to monitor the level of complaints – and their outcomes – as an indicator of school performance.

Absenteeism

In a book entitled *Helping Children Get the Most from School*, it probably goes without saying that the most basic help you can give your child is to see that she actually gets to school each day. Unfortunately, unless you take your child to the school gates and see her walk through the door each day, you can never be absolutely certain that she is actually attending all the time that you think she is. Parents occasionally get a nasty surprise when they are informed that their child has been absent from school on a regular basis, completely unbeknown to them.

Most LEAs employ education welfare officers (or education social workers) whose job it is to monitor school attendance and to help parents meet their responsibilities. If a child is not attending school regularly, the education welfare officer will usually visit her parents to talk about the problem. In persistent cases of truancy, the LEA can ask the court for an education supervision order, appointing an officer to supervise your child's school attendance, and can prosecute parents whose children do not attend school. Fines of up to £1,000 can be imposed on parents whose children do not attend school regularly.

If you find that your child has been absent from school when you thought she was attending, it is important to investigate the reasons for her absence. Children who are being persistently bullied or who have problems with schoolwork that have not been recognized or addressed may find it almost impossible to force themselves into school each day, and children who have worries or emotional problems on their minds may also find school intolerable. Older children who are simply not motivated to continue their education may see no point in being at school when they could be doing something more interesting, and this is another good reason for involving children as far as possible in the choice of school and decisions about whether to stay on post-16 or not.

If there are problems at school that are making it hard for your child to attend, your first step to re-establishing attendance must be to tackle these. If no cause can be found, it is important that parents and school co-operate closely to monitor attendance, and in providing motivation for the child to attend school regularly (see Chapter 3).

Bullying

Studies have shown that one in four children will be involved in bullying at school, as bully or victim, and one of the biggest worries for many parents is that their child will be bullied. Studies have also suggested that incidents of bullying are not the occasional, one-off flare-ups that we would like to believe. In fact, the majority of cases of bullying uncovered by several research projects into discipline and behaviour at school lasted for 12 months or more.

Although it was considered a perfectly normal part of growing up until the latter part of the 1990s, bullying is now acknowledged to be a serious problem, and one which affects children's levels of achievement at school and damages their self-esteem, sometimes for life. Unfortunately, children rarely tell their parents that they are being bullied. Many bullies will warn their victims not to, and the embarrassment of the situation being made public to their classmates, and perhaps the whole school, sometimes outweighs the misery of the bullying itself. The sort of anxiety that results from bullying can't be completely hidden, though, and most parents will be well aware that something has gone wrong in their child's life. Any of the following may indicate that a child is being bullied, although there may be other causes.

- *Withdrawal*
  The bullied child may become quiet and withdrawn, to the point of appearing sullen. He may find it difficult to do anything positive at all, and spend most of his time at home apparently daydreaming or playing computer games, where he can leave behind his doubts about his own ability to cope, and be someone else for a while. Family outings, out-of-school activities and visits to friends may become an ordeal, and the child may prefer to stay at home alone.

- *Becoming difficult and argumentative*
  He may have an exaggerated awareness of any unfairness or favouritism within the family, and feel victimized and put-upon in circumstances where this is clearly not the case. He may resent any minor criticism or demand on his time out of all proportion to the event. A request to tidy his room, for instance, may provoke a flood of tears and protests of 'You're always going on at me – you never tell anyone else to tidy their room!', although this is patently untrue. Underlying these responses is the feeling that 'Everyone's picking on me!'

- *Aggressive behaviour*
  He may 'act out' his anger and frustration by behaving aggressively towards brothers and sisters, or children outside the family. He may pick fights, become overly possessive of toys or food, or overreact to the normal, everyday arguments that are an inevitable part of family life. In an attempt to re-establish his damaged self-esteem and confidence, the victim may become a bully himself.

- *Fear of going to school*
  If the bullying is taking place at school, or on the way there, he may refuse to go, ask repeatedly to be driven rather than walking or catching the bus, or develop frequent mystery illnesses that necessitate his staying at home. Some children will develop full-blown school phobia, where the prospect of going to school is so terrifying that the child will beg, plead, threaten and even become physically ill if his parents insist he goes.

- *School work problems*
  Children who are being bullied at school may spend all their time there in a state of fear and apprehension, and not surprisingly their school work may suffer.

- *Missing possessions*
  School books may be damaged or lost and dinner money and other possessions may go missing. Sometimes the victim of bullying will try to placate the bully by giving him presents of toys, sweets or money. He may offer implausible excuses for loss or damage to his property.

- *Nightmares and disturbed sleep*
  The bullied child may have nightmares, and delay bedtime as long as possible, knowing that his fears will catch up with him while his guard is down. Disturbed sleep will leave him tired in the morning, and it will be quite an effort to get him off to school on time – particularly as school may be the last place he wants to be.
- *Bed-wetting*
  Bed-wetting is often a sign of anxiety, and bullying is always worth considering as a possible cause.
- *Stealing*
  The child who is the victim of a 'protection racket' may have to steal to satisfy the bully's demands. He may become involved in criminal activity, such as shoplifting, because of threats from other children, or the fear of rejection by the group if they don't.
- *Injuries*
  A child who is being bullied physically may have obvious bruises which he will try to explain away. Injuries incurred in school time and reported to staff, in a PE lesson for instance, will be recorded in the school accident book, along with their cause and any treatment given, so it is possible to ask the school to check up on your child's explanations if you suspect that suspiciously frequent injuries may have been inflicted by another child at or outside school.
- *Low self-esteem*
  The victim of verbal bullying may try desperately to change the attributes that the bullies have picked upon for ridicule, asking for a different style of shoes or clothing, or becoming painfully self-conscious about some aspect of her appearance. Some children deliberately fail in their schoolwork after being called 'teacher's pet', others resort to obsessive washing after being called 'smelly' or 'dirty'.
- *Regression*
  An unhappy or frightened child may revert to earlier patterns of behaviour, taking several steps backwards in his development. Younger children may literally wet themselves during

the day with anxiety, while older children may wet the bed. Thumb-sucking, nail-biting, overeating, clinginess, stammering and habits like chewing clothing or bedding are all signs of anxiety which may be caused or contributed to by bullying.

- *Depression*
  Children, like adults, can and do become truly depressed. Lethargy, tearfulness, difficulty in concentrating, loss of appetite or compulsive eating and a tendency to overreact to the slightest setback are all symptoms of depression. Depression, with or without threats of suicide should always be taken seriously (see Chapter 5). The depressed or suicidal child needs urgent help – forcing him to school will only make matters worse.

Any or all of the above could indicate that your child is being bullied, but most of them could be caused by a variety of other worries, so how will you know if bullying is at the root of your child's problem? First, and most importantly, you can encourage your child to talk to you about what is worrying him. This isn't easy at the best of times, and can become more difficult as children get older.

Bullying is an emotive issue, laden for both parent and child with fears of inadequacy, rejection and failure. This can make it a difficult and embarrassing topic of conversation for both, particularly where older children are concerned. Parents who have been bullied themselves may be especially panic-stricken at the thought of their children suffering as they did, and feel extremely uncomfortable about discussing bullying with them, even in a general context. Children are extraordinarily sensitive to these sorts of feelings, and will quickly learn that bullying-related worries are off-limits as far as their parents are concerned. Similarly, parents who have experienced bullying may be quick to interpret normal disagreements and fallings-out between children as bullying, and communicate their concern to their child.

Parental concern about bullying is justified and valuable. Knowing the dangers and understanding what bullying feels like can help you to make the right decisions when choosing your child's schools and activities, encouraging friendships and interpreting his reactions. If your concern makes it difficult to talk to your child in a supportive way about his own experiences, though, it is worth giving some thought to what it is about the subject of bullying that upsets you so much, and trying to separate your own fears from your child's experiences. Talking to someone often helps.

If you feel that something is wrong, but are finding it difficult to talk to your child, try talking to him about bullying in a general way. Tell him about a time when you or a friend were bullied as a child, and what you did about it. Make up a story if necessary, or use one of the excellent children's books covering this issue.

Talk to the school

If you think that your child is being bullied, or is bullying, it is vitally important that you contact the school as soon as possible. Every school should have an anti-bullying policy that describes how it will deal with incidents of bullying, and should bring this into operation as soon as a bullying incident is reported.

Your first point of contact is your child's form teacher. He or she will usually know your child, and often the other children involved as well, and is in the best position to assess the situation and suggest remedies (although this may not always be the case in secondary school, where the class tutor sometimes only sees his/her class for registration, and may not teach them at all). Ask him to:

- investigate your child's complaints;
- keep you informed of the results;
- inform the head teacher of your meeting.

It is important that you go along to the interview with your child's teacher armed with as much information as possible. Don't rely on your memory – write down all the facts you have gathered so far and all the questions you want to ask, or you are certain to miss something out. From the first moment you suspect that bullying may be a problem, either you or your child should keep a detailed diary of events, including:

- names of any children involved, including witnesses;
- dates and times of incidents;
- where the incidents took place;
- details of injuries and any treatment received for them;
- details of damage to or theft of property.

After each meeting, write to those involved confirming the main points covered and detailing any action agreed upon.

What can I expect the school to do?

- Take the matter seriously.
- Protect your child until the matter can be sorted out.
- Talk to the victim, the bully and witnesses.
- Talk to parents of the bully and of bullied children.
- Take action to prevent further bullying.

She doesn't want to tell

Often parents only find out about bullying in a roundabout way, perhaps from another child or parent. Or they may suspect that their child is being bullied but have no concrete proof. In these cases, you may be unable to provide much in the way of evidence to back up your concerns. Don't be put off by the school saying that it is impossible for them to take action without evidence. Names and details make investigation easier, of course, but even if it proves impossible for the school to track down the culprits in this particular incident, there is much that they can do to discourage bullying generally. Even a general warning to the whole school, if made with sufficient conviction and carried through, can be very effective.

If you don't feel that your school is doing enough to prevent bullying, or to protect your child, follow the complaints procedure outlined earlier in this chapter. Do not hesitate to keep your child away from school if you (or she) feel that she is not safe there. Most schools will advise against this, rightly asserting that the longer she stays away, the more difficult it will be for her to return. This is all well and good if they can assure you that your child will be protected from bullying while she is at school and as she arrives and leaves. If they can't, or if promises of protection are not fulfilled, there is absolutely no point in forcing a distressed and frightened child back into school for another day of fear and anticipation. She will learn nothing and the damage caused by the bullying will get steadily more difficult to reverse.

For further information on preventing and dealing with bullying, see my book *Helping Children Cope with Bullying* (see p. 143 for details).

What if the bully's a teacher?

Some teachers still use fear, taunts and humiliation to control their classes. Sometimes a teacher will take a dislike to a particular child, and belittle everything she does, labelling her lazy, badly behaved, or just plain thick. Because children and parents expect teachers to use their authority responsibly, this form of bullying may not be recognized as such, although it is potentially extremely damaging to the child.

If you suspect that your child is being bullied by a particular teacher, perhaps because she has complained to you about it, because she is obviously distressed before or after a particular class, or because you have heard about it from other children or parents, the best approach in the first instance is probably to talk to the teacher concerned. Don't accuse him or her of bullying your child, simply say that you are concerned about how she is getting on and want to ask the teacher's advice. You may be able to gauge his or her attitude by the way he or she responds to your concerns.

If a teacher is bullying your child or others, the situation must be brought to the attention of the school. Often, teachers will be aware of a colleague's methods, but it takes complaints by children and parents to get anything done. A good school will listen to your worries and take action – in the secondary school attended by my own children, a teacher was sacked after complaints from parents, and the reason for his dismissal made known to the children. This went a long way towards reversing the damage he had done to some individuals, and to increase the children's confidence in the fairness and sincerity of the school's anti-bullying policy.

Bad behaviour at school

Some parents will know only too well that their child can be difficult to handle. If you know this about your child, it is important for you to talk to his teacher in advance and to work out with her a consistent approach to his behaviour. Sometimes, however, it will come as a complete and unpleasant surprise to hear unfavourable reports about your child's behaviour at school.

We all have to accept that we don't know everything about our children, and when it comes to their behaviour when we are not around we can only do our best to show them what is acceptable and what is not, and then keep our fingers crossed. There are many other influences on a child's behaviour, including peer pressure, emotional and physical environment and health, and inborn differences in the ability to cope with stress and frustration. Situations that one child can sail through with equanimity will leave another anxious, furious or demoralized, despite the best efforts of his parents to put him on the right track. In short, if you are told by the school that there are concerns about your child's behaviour, listen with an open mind, even if it sounds out of character. If there is a problem, you need to know about it in order to be able to help your child. Denying that there is a problem at all won't make it go away.

- Listen to all that your child's teacher has to say, and ask for all the details she can give you. Was this a sudden, one-off aberration, or has your child's behaviour been deteriorating over a long period? Were there other children involved? Did the teacher you're speaking to witness this event, or was it reported by someone else? If so, who? Does your child's teacher have any idea what is causing your child to misbehave? Is he coping well with school work? Try to get all the background possible before you talk to your child.

- Ask your child about what has been happening at school. Don't go in with all guns blazing – say that his teacher is concerned about his behaviour and ask what he feels about it. Encourage him to tell you how he feels about the situation or incident, and ask him how he thinks he can avoid it happening again/getting worse. Try to arrive at some positive conclusion with your child, and agree an action plan for the future.

- Talk to your child's teacher again, perhaps with your child, and explain what you have talked over and what your child has undertaken to do for the future. Agree that you will both monitor the situation, and contact each other if there is anything to report.

Sanctions

On the whole, rewards work better than threats. Rather than saying to your child, 'I'll take away one of your toys for every bad report I get from school', which will simply make her feel sullen and put-upon, try saying, 'If you manage to keep up this improvement, let's all go out to Alton Towers to celebrate at half-term.' Most important of all, make it clear to your child that it is her behaviour that you dislike, not her.

The school will have its own system of punishments for bad behaviour, ranging from detention, through being 'on report', to the ultimate sanction, exclusion. If you think that your child has been wrongly accused, you must of course dispute their decision to punish her. Otherwise, help her to see that she belongs to a community with its own established and well-understood rules, and that in order for that community to function everybody must abide by those rules, even if they don't fully agree with all of them. The way to deal with rules you believe are wrong is to try to get them changed, not to flout them, and most secondary schools will have a school council or its equivalent, through which pupils can have their views on school policy represented. If she does break a rule, she can expect to be punished for it just as anyone else would – that is part of being a member of a social group.

Exclusion

As a last resort, your child's head teacher can decide to exclude her from school on disciplinary grounds. He or she must tell you why your child is being excluded, and how long the exclusion will last. In really serious cases, your child can be excluded from the school permanently. This sanction is usually reserved for persistent offenders, or for children who have done something extremely serious that would bring the school into disrepute, like selling drugs to other pupils.

If your child is excluded, you have the right to appeal to the governors' discipline committee, and then to an independent appeal panel in the case of permanent exclusion. If the appeal panel decides against your child, the only recourse left to parents is a judicial review, or to the Local Government Ombudsman if the panel didn't conduct the hearing properly. The Secretary of State for Education cannot overturn the decision of an independent appeal panel.

Exam results

If you feel that your child has been wrongly graded in a public examination (not an internal school examination, but GCSEs or A levels), you can ask the school to query the grades with the relevant examination board. If, having been through the awarding body's appeals procedure, you and the school feel that your child has still been unfairly graded, the school can appeal to the Examination Appeals Board – but only if they believe that the awarding body's procedures have not been followed or are at fault. The Examinations Appeals Board cannot 're-mark' the examination.

If your child has not done as well as you and she would like in a public examination, and the school does not want to re-enter her, you have the right to re-enter her for the examination yourself, provided you are willing to pay the re-entry fee. You can also ask to see your child's marked examination papers, 'for general interest or to inform future learning'. If you would like to do this, you should ask the school for advice on how to make your request.

9

The Gifted Child and the Underachiever

At first sight, it may seem odd to lump the gifted child and the underachiever into the same chapter – aren't their experiences of education and the support they need from parents and school very different? In fact, it is often the very gifted child who makes the most difficult pupil, and where a child is having problems at school the possibility that he is of unusually high ability should always be considered.

Is your child gifted?

It is all too easy to damage the self-confidence of a very bright or gifted child, and it is in the interests of all concerned that such children are identified as early as possible in their school career. Parents will often know well before their child starts school, from comparisons with other children or siblings, that he is of above average ability, and it is important that this information is passed on to the school, as it will affect the way that he is taught.

The National Association for Gifted Children provides the following checklist of some of the common characteristics of gifted children.

The gifted child:

- asks lots of questions and learns more quickly than others;
- has a very retentive memory;
- is extremely curious and can concentrate for long periods on subjects of interest;
- has a wide general knowledge and interest in the world;
- enjoys problem-solving, often missing out the intermediate stages in an argument and making original connections;
- has an unusual imagination;

- shows strong feelings and opinions and has an odd sense of humour;
- sets high standards and is a perfectionist.

Good schools will try to identify their more able pupils, and to meet their needs, but this is not always easy. Unfortunately, the issue can be complicated by other characteristics that often seem to go hand in hand with exceptional ability.

- *Poor hand–eye co-ordination*
  Some children who are very quick at logic and problem-solving may find writing difficult, and can become so disheartened that they refuse to write at all. This problem is thought to be related to brain structure.
- *Difficulty expressing themselves in words*
  Some children show outstanding mechanical and artistic ability, but are not good at talking and listening.
- *ADHD, dyslexia and dyspraxia*
  These conditions are often associated with high intelligence and giftedness. Attention deficit hyperactivity disorder (ADHD, or ADD where there is no hyperactivity component) is a condition in which the child has difficulty in maintaining attention and concentration, controlling impulsive behaviour and controlling their physical activity. Dyslexia is a specific type of learning difficulty where a person of normal intelligence has persistent and significant problems with reading, writing, spelling and sometimes mathematics and musical notation. Dyspraxic children have co-ordination problems that make them appear clumsy, and they find it hard to organize themselves and their work. They may also have difficulties with communication.
  Children with these conditions are often highly intelligent, but their abilities may be missed because they are masked by their problems. Children with these conditions can become the subject of a statement of special needs, but the help they are allocated will address their behaviour problems, not their need for intellectual stimulation.

- *Poor IQ scores*
  Some children who are particularly gifted in the fields of imagination and creativity may not do well in traditional intelligence tests, which are not designed to assess these areas.

Because they may be behind their classmates in some areas, gifted children are often not recognized as such by their teachers, and as a result their special educational needs are not met. They become frustrated with their lack of ability to perform tasks that their classmates find easy, and bored by work that fails to capture their imagination and stretch their knowledge-thirsty intelligence. These children can then become demotivated, difficult and unhappy at school. They might:

- try to avoid going to school;
- go in for tantrums and sulks;
- be disruptive and awkward when they are at school;
- switch off at school, daydream, refuse to do work and make mistakes when the subject does not challenge them;
- have difficulty in mixing with their classmates;
- see no point in doing certain pieces of work, and ask awkward questions of the teacher.

Some gifted children will try to hide their abilities, because they mark them out as different from other children and may attract bullying. They may be seen by other pupils and, unfortunately, by teachers as 'clever-dicks' or 'bigheads' when they know the answers to all the questions, or see inconsistencies that the teacher has missed. Because of this, they can sometimes spend their whole school career masquerading as an 'average' child, and never reaching their full potential. For this group, home education – in which the child is free to explore subjects to the limits of his interest and ability – can be a real advantage (see Chapter 10).

What can the school do to help?

Most teachers and head teachers will acknowledge that it is very difficult to cater for the gifted child in school. Because unusually high ability is not seen as a 'special educational need', extra funding to support the learning of these children is not available to schools (perversely, though, they may receive funded help for the behavioural difficulties that can arise from the failure to meet their needs).

It is obviously very difficult for a teacher who is already overburdened by the educational system with record-keeping and testing, and struggling to meet the needs of a large class, to come up with a separate but complementary programme of activities for one child, without any extra resources. Often, the gifted child is moved up the school more quickly than others, but this is not an ideal solution. Although he may be intellectually precocious, he can be emotionally and developmentally less mature even than other children of his own age, and this gap becomes more obvious when he is moved into the company of children older than himself. The child can feel even more different and isolated, confidence can be damaged, and he will need lots of support at home and school to cope with the problems that can arise.

What can you do to help?

If you believe that your child may be unusually able:

- Choose a school that has a clear policy on providing for gifted children.
- Talk to his teacher about his strengths and weaknesses before he starts school, or a new class.
- Ask for your child to be assessed by an educational psychologist if you feel that the school has not recognized his abilities (you may have to arrange and fund this yourself, as resources are overstretched).
- Provide mental stimulation for him at home.
- Watch for signs of boredom or frustration at school, and liaise with his teacher.
- Contact one or more support groups for families with gifted children.
- Consider home education.

Above all, don't forget that he is a child. It is very easy, faced with a child who is obviously streets ahead of the others in some respect, to focus on this one area of his life to the exclusion of the rest. Growing up is all about becoming a balanced individual, and we neglect our children's emotional, physical and spiritual needs at our (or rather their) peril.

It gives us very good feelings about ourselves as parents to see our children do well, but be very careful that your child doesn't come to see his talent as the only worthwhile thing about him – both to you and to others. Many talented children have turned away from the activity at which they excel because they want to test whether their worst fears – that their parents only love them for what they can do, not for what they are – are true.

The underachiever

A child is described as underachieving at school when she is not reaching her full potential for learning. If you are concerned that your child is underachieving, the first question to ask is whether your expectations of her are realistic. Not all children will be academic stars. Some children's talents will be in other directions – creativity, the ability to do skilled work with their hands, a gift for working with animals or children, and so on. These children may struggle a bit at school, or plod along consistently getting unremarkable results, but will not shine until they have found the setting in life that brings out the best in them. They cannot really be said to be underachieving, however, and it would be far better for their parents to put some effort into finding their strengths outside school than to ruin their confidence by pushing them to reach unrealistic goals. If you feel that your child is underachieving, ask yourself the following questions.

- Is she happy at school?
- Are you giving her the support outlined in this book?
- Is her behaviour generally good?
- Does the school work she is doing 'stretch' her intellectual capacity?

- Does she work consistently?
- Are her teachers happy with her progress?

If your answer to these questions is largely 'yes', then your child is probably not underachieving. If, however, you know that your child is not fully engaged by her time at school, that she has capacity that she is not using, or that she shows signs of being unhappy with and unsatisfied by school, then it is important that you talk to her and to her teachers about your worries.

Reasons for underachieving

As we have seen, some underachievers are exceptionally bright children who are just not sufficiently 'stretched' by the normal school curriculum. Once their abilities have been recognized, the school can try to provide a programme of work that the child will find more satisfying and stimulating. For others, there may be an unrecognized physical, psychological or developmental problem underlying their underachievement. These might include:

- problems with eyesight or hearing;
- undiagnosed illness;
- emotional problems or worries that make concentration on school work difficult;
- conditions such as dyslexia, ADHD, dyspraxia and others.

It is important that any underlying condition is recognized as soon as possible. See Chapter 11 for information on investigating and getting help for your child's problems.

Comparisons

Comparisons with classmates can be an unreliable method of assessing your child's abilities, particularly early on in his school career. Children mature at different rates, and while one 5-year-old will be able to read a few words even before starting school, another may not have reached this stage in his development until he has been at school for several months, or even a year. This says nothing about the relative intelligence or potential of the two children under comparison, and the slower starter may well go on to outstrip others in his class as he moves up the school. Try to look at your child as an individual first, using comparisons only as a general guide to his overall stage of development.

The less academic child

Academic achievement is not all-important. Even a university degree no longer assures its holder of a job, and many people with no academic qualifications whatever go on to have satisfying and successful careers. A basic education, however, is useful, and if your child is not particularly academic it is important that her lack of obvious success doesn't put her off the whole educational process, and destroy her confidence in her own abilities. It is all too easy for schools, struggling with a results-driven system, to neglect the needs of such children, although a good school will find ways of showing them that they are valued as much as the more academic high-achievers. Parents, however, can do a tremendous amount to help their less academic children to get the most out of school, and life in general. As well as following the more general advice in this book, if your child is unlikely to shine at school:

- Try hard to find activities that she can excel at, and encourage her to keep them up.
- Recognize all her achievements at school and outside, however small.
- Don't compare her unfavourably with others.
- Show her clearly that you love her for who she is, not what she does.

10

Home Education – An Alternative?

Who educates at home?

Home education is on the increase. There are many reasons for parents deciding to opt out of the school system, including:

- bullying at school;
- school phobia;
- a gifted child who can't be catered for in school;
- dissatisfaction with a child's progress;
- religious or philosophical requirements that cannot be met at available schools;
- health problems or disabilities that make local schools unsuitable.

The law in England and Wales does not oblige you to send your child to school. It simply states that she must be educated, and that it is the parents' responsibility to see that she is. This is clearly established in the 1996 Education Act, which states that:

> The parent of every child of compulsory school age shall cause him to receive efficient full-time education suitable;
>
> a) to his age, ability, and aptitude, and
> b) to any special educational needs he may have, either by regular attendance at school or otherwise.

The Northern Ireland Act of 1947 contains a section identical to this, while the Scottish Education Act of 1962 contains a similar section.

It's your choice

It is your responsibility as a parent to ensure that your child is properly educated, and the decision whether to use schools to that end or to educate your child at home is entirely yours. You do not need anyone's permission, nor do you have to justify your decision to anyone. You are not even obliged to inform your LEA of your intention to educate your child at home unless she is already registered at a state school. If your child is already registered, you must write to the head of the school to tell him or her of your intention to withdraw your child. Your child will be de-registered automatically, and you are not required to justify your decision. It is then the head's responsibility to inform the LEA of your child's withdrawal.

What qualifications will you need?

You do not need any qualifications to educate your child at home. No special equipment is required, you need not cover the National Curriculum or provide the authorities with timetables, work plans or a specific syllabus.

Jane's three children, aged 8, 7 and 4, have been home educated for 18 months:

> I wondered whether I, with six O levels and nothing more, would be able to teach them. I have found that I actually have to teach very little, it is quite impossible to prevent a happy, self-directed child from learning. Once they left school they found that learning is fun when it's not called 'work', and I settled into my role of facilitator and adviser.

Anne has been educating her son Christopher (13) at home for two years:

> Home educating one's child seems a big step to take at first – you feel you are stepping out of line, entering unknown territory, and need to be the fount of all knowledge and ideas in order to fulfil your child's needs. It can seem like a daunting task, which I think stems from our own (mostly schooled) experiences that all education comes from being taught.
>
> We started out re-creating school at home, but very soon our

son actually guided us, through his innate ability to know what his needs were, towards autonomous learning. Now we understand so much better how we all learn, all we need to do is respect him and trust him to teach himself, just as he learned as a baby to walk and talk. I am constantly amazed at how much information he picks up along the way, without our having to do anything at all other than support and encourage him.

Anne's son, Christopher, agrees:

I started by doing subjects, but I didn't like that much and now I learn autonomously. I like this much better because I can choose what I do and I don't have to sit down and learn from books unless I want to. When I was at school I didn't have much time to myself. Even when I got home I had to do homework. I hated that. Now I do lots of different things. I recently took part in making a TV programme – that was great.

Do home-educated children miss out socially?

One of the most common concerns of parents who are considering home educating is that their child will miss out on regular contact with others. This is not seen as a problem by those who are engaged in home education. Although children at school come into contact with many others of their own age, they tend to make close friendships with only a few of them, and as long as your child has the opportunity to meet people of all ages, he will choose those he wants to spend more time with for himself. In many areas, home educators form local groups and get together for field trips, study and social events, giving their children a chance to meet.

Jane: I actually think that the biggest benefit of HE is the social aspect! My children are out and about in the real world, watching and joining in with adults going about their lives,

119

treating each other as equals, having confrontations and disputes and reaching agreement amicably without a figure of artificial authority stepping in to place blame and impose discipline. They are free to question and discuss the rules of society.

We have a thriving home-ed group, meeting up two or three times a week for social/educational activities: weekly gym, fortnightly drama (because the demand was so high we run two groups on alternate weeks), monthly swimming, monthly ramble, monthly activity afternoon in community centre, monthly trip to museum/gallery/zoo/outward bound centre, etc. Many of us also meet up in between with particular friends too. We are lucky to have an HE family round the corner but the girls also play with local schoolchildren in the evenings and at weekends.

Because the school environment is so different from any that we experience in adult life, being at school probably only teaches us (in social terms) how to function at school. For children who will not attend school, this could be seen as an irrelevant skill.

Christopher: People always ask if I miss the other children. I don't miss them at all, most weren't very nice anyway. I do have friends and I play a lot, and now I meet lots of different people.

Christopher's mother agrees:

Christopher's experiences at school were largely *anti*-social. I feel that our son has benefited enormously from *not* having to mix with children (and adults, for that matter) at school who seem to have adopted a culture of bullying and being deliberately nasty to each other. He has been able to choose his friends, some of whom are younger, some older, some are adults. He is not forced to spend too much time with people who make him feel uncomfortable. He has developed a great deal of self-confidence since being out of school and I truly believe his social skills to be developing much better than if he was still in school.

Help for parents

Education Otherwise, a self-help organization formed by a group of parents in the 1970s, offers support, advice and information to families interested in or practising home-based education as an alternative to schooling for their children. EO's members have found that local education authority officials, who have a duty to ensure that an 'efficient' and 'suitable' education is being provided for any child not attending school, are usually sympathetic and co-operative in their dealings with parents who have decided to educate their children at home, although there are exceptions. In the event of a serious dispute arising the LEA may pass the matter on to the magistrate's court, so it is advisable for any parent contemplating educating a child at home to contact either EO or the Children's Home-Based Education Association (see Useful Addresses for details) for advice on presenting their case to the LEA. Once a child is engaged in home education, the LEA will send an Inspector to monitor his progress from time to time.

Education Otherwise stresses that you don't have to be a teacher to educate your child – in fact the majority of home educators have no formal qualifications. You don't have to work to a timetable, and you are not obliged to follow the National Curriculum, although you may do so if you wish. Neither is choosing to educate your child at home necessarily a once-and-for-all decision. Sometimes a period at home can give the child a chance to regain self-esteem and self-confidence, and then go back into school again with renewed confidence and hope.

11
Special Needs

Most schools do an excellent job of assessing and allowing for the individual needs of the children in their care. Sometimes, though, a child has needs that are beyond the scope of an ordinary school to provide for from their normal resources.

What are special educational needs?

A child who, because of a physical, mental, emotional or behavioural problem, finds it much harder to learn than most children of the same age, is described as having special educational needs (SEN). A child whose disability makes it difficult for her to use the normal educational facilities in the area also has special educational needs. The local education authority is bound to provide extra help for any child who is assessed as having such a need, and does so through the statutory assessment and statement of special educational needs process.

A statement of special educational needs is not just for the child who is physically or mentally handicapped. Children who have a temporary need for extra help, perhaps because of emotional or behavioural problems, or difficulties with specific skills such as reading or writing, can also benefit from a statement, which can be removed once the need has passed.

A statement should never be seen by parents as an admission of failure, or as branding their child as somehow defective. The DfES estimates that 1 in 50 children will have a special educational need at some time during their school years, and the vast majority of these will, with a little extra temporary or longer-term help, go on to have a successful and happy school career, often continuing into further education.

The law says that children with special educational needs should be educated in mainstream schools wherever possible, and allows for extra help to be provided within the school to this end, or for a place in a special school to be provided where integration into a normal school is not possible.

The pre-school child

If you feel that your pre-school child has a developmental or health problem that may later affect her schooling, it is very important that you talk as early as possible to your doctor or health visitor, who can refer your child to the LEA. It may take some time to get help, and even before they start school or playgroup, children are learning the skills they will need to build on at school. The LEA can provide help for your pre-school child – for example:

- teachers who will visit your home if your child has hearing or sight problems, or learning difficulties;
- home-based learning schemes in which a trained home visitor helps you by suggesting activities that will encourage your child to develop new skills;
- playgroups and opportunity groups that can help your child develop socially and through play.

The primary and secondary schoolchild

Every school must have a written policy describing, among other things:

- how the school will identify children who need special help;
- how that help will be delivered, stage by stage;
- how the school will involve the parents of children with special needs;
- who the school's special educational needs co-ordinator is;
- how complaints will be handled.

If you know before your child starts primary school that she will need extra help, ask to see the special needs policy of any school you are considering for her. You can also ask for an interview with the school's special needs coordinator before you make your choice, and talk to the parents of other children with SEN already at the school. This may materially affect your choice of school for your child.

When problems arise at school

Often parents, health visitors or pre-school staff will have noticed very early on that a child is having problems, but sometimes it is only when the child starts school that it becomes apparent that she needs extra help. A problem may develop during a child's time at primary school, and occasionally it is not until secondary school that a need is identified. Let's examine the steps most schools go through when a pupil is identified as having special needs:

1 You or your child's teacher become concerned about her progress at school

If you feel that your child is having difficulties of any sort at school, your first step is to talk to her. Once you have found out all you can from your child, the next step is to ask to talk to her teacher or form tutor. Tell the teacher about anything that may be affecting your child's school experience, including anything she has told you or that you have noticed about her time at school, her health and development generally, her behaviour outside school and any family problems that may be troubling her. It may help if you note down before the meeting the things you wish to mention.

Your child's teacher should be able to tell you about her behaviour at school, her relationships with other children and how she seems to be coping with the work she is doing. He may be able to set your mind at rest straightaway, but if this is not the case he may suggest ways in which your child can be helped over what may be a temporary hiccup in her education, perhaps by providing a little extra help at school or at home until she has caught up. In this case, it is wise to set a specified time period after which you will meet again to assess the success of these measures. Make a note in your diary, and follow up with a request for another appointment when the allotted time has passed.

Your child's teacher may feel that there just isn't a problem. Bear in mind that teachers see a great many children, and have a very good idea of what is normal for your child's age group and stage of development. Listen carefully to what the teacher has to say, but if you still feel that there is an unrecognized problem that is holding your child back and the teacher does not agree, you should ask to speak to the head teacher or head of year.

If the measures you and your child's teacher have decided on do not bring about the desired improvement, the next stage is to provide more structured help within the school.

2   Your school's SEN coordinator is involved

Every school has a SEN coordinator, in most cases a member of the teaching staff who has taken on the additional responsibility of overseeing the school's provision for all its pupils with special educational needs, whether they have been assessed and statemented or not. She will have had extra training in special needs issues, and can arrange training for other members of staff.

This teacher will talk both to you and to your child's teacher/s, and then draw up an individual education plan. This plan will set targets for your child to achieve, and schedule a review when her progress will be assessed. You should have an opportunity to see the SEN coordinator and discuss the draft plan once it has been prepared.

Your child's progress will be assessed regularly, and the plan will be revised accordingly. Extra help at this stage will be provided from within the school's existing resources – the teacher or a classroom helper may spend extra time with your child in class, for instance. Inevitably the more time they give your child the less they give to the others in the class. This can cause problems for teachers, particularly if there are several children in the school who need extra help.

The school should keep you in touch with your child's

progress, and it would be a good idea to make a note in your diary of the assessment dates mentioned in the plan, and ask for a meeting with your child's teacher if he doesn't keep you informed. If this approach doesn't seem to be working, the school will probably suggest that they call in some outside help. If they don't, you can ask them to do so.

3 The school calls in a specialist such as an educational psychologist or specialist teacher

If your child's needs are not being met by the individual education plan set out by the school, the SEN coordinator may call in a specialist from outside the school who will help to draw up a new plan. Again, progress will be assessed at regular intervals, and you should be kept informed and invited into school to review your child's progress. If this approach does not produce the desired result, the head teacher must decide whether to ask the LEA to make a statutory assessment of your child's special educational needs.

4 The head teacher asks the LEA to make a statutory assessment

Any extra help given to a child who has not had a statement of SEN has to come from within the existing resources of the school, so most head teachers will be keen to apply for a statutory assessment where they think there is a reasonable chance of getting one.

If your school is reluctant to apply for a statutory assessment of your child's needs, another professional involved with your child, such as a doctor, can ask the LEA for an assessment. You can ask for an assessment yourself if you feel that your child is falling seriously behind other children of the same age, and that her school cannot provide the extra help she needs, but it is wise to keep this as a last resort, as a request from your school will carry much more weight.

Whoever has made the application for an assessment, the LEA is obliged to keep you in touch with the decision-making process.

The DfES requires that the LEA take no more than six weeks from the date of application to tell you whether or not they will make a statutory assessment of your child, and that they should explain any delay. If you are not happy with the LEA's reasons for such a delay, your last resort is the Secretary of State for Education, who can direct the LEA to resolve the problem.

If the LEA refuses to assess your child, they must write to you and the school giving the reasons for their decision, and you have the right to appeal to the Special Educational Needs Tribunal (SENT) if you disagree. Any appeal has to be made within two months of the LEA's decision.

5   *An assessment is made, and the LEA decides whether to make a statement of special needs, based on its findings*

This process should take no more than 12 weeks from the decision to make an assessment. The LEA may decide that your child can be provided for in school without a statement. Again, you can appeal against this decision to the SENT.

You have the right to go with your child to any interview, medical or other test during the statutory assessment. The LEA may ask your child what she thinks about her special educational needs, and if she needs help in giving these views you, a teacher or another person of your choice can help.

6   *A statement is made and either a place in a special school or extra help and resources in a mainstream school are provided*

The LEA will decide that a statement is necessary for your child only if they feel that all the special help she needs cannot reasonably be provided within the resources, including money, staff time and equipment, normally available to the school. The statement itself will describe your child's learning difficulties, as identified by the assessment, the special help she needs, the long-term objectives of that help and the arrangements that will be made for setting short-term targets and assessing her progress. It will also give details of the school that she will attend, and describe any non-educational needs your child has, such as transport to school, and how these needs will be met.

Before the statement is finalized, you will receive a draft copy of the document, and copies of all the advice the LEA got from you and from others during the statutory assessment. At this stage you will be able to choose the school you wish your child to attend. The LEA must go along with this choice as long as:

- the school you choose is suitable for your child's age, ability and special educational needs;
- your child's presence there will not affect the efficient education of other children already at the school;
- placing your child in the school will be an efficient use of the LEA's resources.

The LEA may fund your child's attendance at an independent or non-maintained school (one that charges fees or is funded by a charity, rather than a state school), but is unlikely to do so if there is a suitable state school in your area. You can, of course, choose the school your child is already attending.

Once the choice of school has been made, and within eight weeks of the proposed statement, the final statement is prepared, and comes into force straightaway. The LEA must then provide your child's school with any necessary extra resources identified in the statement. The school's governors have a duty to see that your child gets the help set out in the statement. In practice, however, the help may simply not be available (see Jake's story below).

These steps are laid out in the DfES Code of Practice on the Identification and Assessment of Special Educational Needs, a guidance document for schools and LEAs to which all state schools are obliged legally to 'have regard', although they are not required to follow it to the letter. School can miss out the first three stages, in cases where it is felt that the child needs specialist help, and apply for a statutory assessment straightaway.

In theory, this process, from proposing an assessment to making a statement, takes 26 weeks – less than seven months. In reality, getting funding for extra help for your child can be a

daunting process, and hard-pressed schools are often left struggling to provide for the needs of challenging and demanding
children from their already overstretched resources. In order to
get the best from the system, parents and school will have to
work together, as Jake's story, told below by his mother,
illustrates.

Jake was born prematurely, one of twins, and as a baby was
given drugs to prevent seizures, one effect of which was to
mask his developmental problems. At 4, even though he had
been off the drugs for nearly two years, he was still way
behind his twin sister. Doctors still insisted that this was the
result of the anti-seizure drugs.

Jake started school when he was 5. His reception teacher
was a godsend. She could see that he was a bright boy but she
had trouble understanding his speech, and his writing was
nowhere near the level of a 5-year-old. She asked if he had
attention deficit disorder or Asperger's syndrome, and I said I
wasn't aware that he had.

The school did everything they could within their means to
accommodate him, but it was taxing their resources as they
were providing for his needs without any extra funding. The
head teacher ordered tests with the school nurse. She referred
him to the school doctor who diagnosed dyspraxia then and
there, but Jake had to be referred to speech, occupational and
educational therapists and psychologists in order to produce a
statutory assessment. It took about eight months to get an
appointment with the speech therapist, and then about a year
into the process the occupational therapist saw him. After two
years overall, he was finally statemented, so that by the
September he started Year 3 he was given the help he needed.

Jake now gets five hours' extra help a week at school. The
head teacher was very disappointed with this, as was I, and
called an early review, the result of which is pending. So many
opportunities have been missed because of the long delay in
getting the extra help he needs. He still does not get speech
therapy because they are short staffed and have no one who

can handle his special need. His speech has gone from bad to worse, and it's affecting his self-esteem. The delay with occupational therapy has led to him always sitting on the bench when his friends play football and he still cannot ride his bike without stabilizers – if he had got the occupational therapy sooner he might have achieved that by now.

I have nothing but praise for the school and the head teacher, and especially Jake's reception teacher, who noticed the problem in the first place. It's hard for them to cope because the extra funding they receive is constantly up for review. If the child makes the slightest progress the school must fight to keep the statementing because the LEA argues that it is no longer needed, and can either reduce it or cut it back completely.

There is such a lot to go through – the child has to undergo endless testing and evaluations, even before the statement can begin. In my son's case all the professionals agreed he was not misbehaving, he was not educationally subnormal (his vocabulary is at the level of a 12-year-old) and even then the whole process took over 18 months. He has stopped receiving speech therapy because they don't have the resources and he had to wait two years for occupational therapy.

When Jake does well, though, it's amazing – he takes great pride in his achievements, and I do too. Recently he had to do a report on ancient Egypt. We did it together on the computer. He got the highest grade in class and was so proud. He got a certificate – the school is always encouraging him as he is so easily discouraged. It's been a real struggle to get the help Jake needs, and I am just so thankful that his reception teacher recognized the problem early on.

It is clear from Jake's story that just getting your child's problems recognized by the experts is not enough. Many parents will have to fight long and hard to get their children the help they need, and the backing of the school is essential if they are to succeed.

Useful Addresses

Advisory Centre for Education

www.ace-ed.org.uk

Department A
Unit 1C, Aberdeen Studios
22 Highbury Grove
London N5 2DQ
Tel.: 020 7354 8318
Advice line: 0808 800 5793 (Monday–Friday 2 p.m.–5 p.m.)
Fax: 020 7354 9069
E-mail: ace-ed@easynet.co.uk

News and information for parents, school governors and teachers. ACE produce many useful leaflets and publications, including *Appealing for a School, Tackling Bullying, Getting Extra Help* and *Exclusion*.

Campaign for State Education (CASE)

www.casenet.org.uk

158 Durham Road
London SW20 0DG
Tel./Fax: 020 8944 8206

An education campaign group, which campaigns for the right of all to the highest quality education. Information about all aspects of state education.

ChildcareLink

www.childcarelink.gov.uk

Information about pre-school services throughout England, Scotland and Wales.

Details of local information services and factsheets on pre-school options are available on freephone: 0800 096 0296.

ChildLine

www.childline.org.uk

ChildLine is the UK's free, 24-hour helpline for children and young people in trouble or danger. If you want to talk to someone, call ChildLine free on 0800 1111. The lines can be busy so please keep trying.

Children's Legal Centre

www2.essex.ac.uk/clc

The Children's Legal Centre
University of Essex
Wivenhoe Park
Colchester
Essex CO4 3SQ
Advice line: 01206 873820 (Monday–Friday 10 a.m.–12.30 p.m. and 2 p.m.–4.30 p.m.)
Education legal advocacy unit: 01206 873966
Administration/publications: 01206 872466
Fax: 01206 874026
E-mail: clc@essex.ac.uk

An independent national charity concerned with the law and policy affecting children and young people. Extensive publications list and a legal query service.

Contact-a-Family

www.cafamily.org.uk

209–211 City Road
London EC1V 1JN
Tel.: 020 7608 8700

Fax: 020 7608 8701
Minicom: 020 7608 8702
Freephone helpline for parents and families: 0808 808 3555
(Monday–Friday 10 a.m.–4 p.m.)
E-mail: info@cafamily.org.uk

A charity helping families who care for children with any
disability or special need.

Department for Education and Skills

www.dfes.gov.uk

Sanctuary Buildings
Great Smith Street
London SW1P 3BT
Tel.: 020 7925 5000
Central fax: 020 7925 6000
Public enquiries: 0870 000 2288
Minicom: 020 7925 6873
E-mail: info@dfes.gsi.gov.uk
For Ministers only: dfes.ministers@dfes.gsi.gov.uk

DfES Governors' Centre

www.dfes.gov.uk/governor

Web site providing information for school governors.

DfES Publications Centre

PO Box 5050
Sudbury
Suffolk CO10 6ZQ

For information on many aspects of education, including *Guide
to the special educational needs tribunal*, and *The parents
charter*. Many leaflets are available in Bengali, Chinese, Greek,
Gujerati, Hindi, Punjabi, Turkish, Urdu and Vietnamese. Write

for a publications list, see the DfES web site for parents (www.dfes.gov.uk/parents) or ring the orderline on 0845 602 2260.

Education Otherwise

www.education-otherwise.org

PO Box 7420
London N9 9SG

For urgent help tel.: 0870 730 0074 for recorded details of contacts.

Support for families who are practising or considering education at home. Send an A5 SAE for information.

Home Education Advisory Service

www.heas.org.uk

PO Box 98
Welwyn Garden City
Herts AL8 6AN
Tel.: 01707 371854
Fax: 01707 371854
E-mail: admin@heas.org.uk

Information, advice and practical support relating to home education.

Independent Panel for Special Education Advice

www.ipsea.org.uk

6 Carlow Mews
Woodbridge
Suffolk IP12 1DH
Advice line: 0800 018 4016 or 01394 382814
Tribunal appeals only: 020 8682 0442

General enquiries: 01394 380518
Scotland: 0131 454 0082
Northern Ireland: 01232 705654

Advice on the help available if you are a parent of a child with special needs, and are having problems with their education.

Independent Schools Information Service (ISIS)
www.isis.org.uk

National ISIS
Grosvenor Gardens House
35–37 Grosvenor Gardens
London SW1W 0BS
Tel.: 020 7798 1500
Fax: 020 7798 1531
E-mail: national@isis.org.uk

Information and advice on choosing an independent school for your child.

Local Government Ombudsman

Local Government Ombudsmen investigate complaints of injustice arising from maladministration by local authorities and certain other bodies.

Advice line: 0845 602 1983 (Monday–Friday 9 a.m.–4.30 p.m.)

National Association for Gifted Children
www.nagcbritain.org.uk

Suite 14, Challenge House
Sherwood Drive
Bletchley
Milton Keynes MK3 6DP
Tel.: 0870 770 3217

Advice on identifying and supporting gifted children.

National Confederation of Parent Teacher Associations (NCPTA)

www.ncpta.org.uk

18 St John's Hill
Sevenoaks
Kent TN13 3NP
Tel.: 01732 748850
Fax: 01732 748851

Help, advice and support in running a PTA. Newsletter, magazine and publications for members. Promotes partnerships between home and school; parents and teachers; parents, LEAs and other interested organizations.

National Children's Bureau

www.ncb.org.uk
8 Wakley Street
London EC1V 7QE
Tel.: 020 7843 6000
Fax: 020 7278 9512

A charity that promotes the interests and well-being of all children and young people. Publications, conferences, library and information services.

National Family and Parenting Institute

www.nfpi.org.uk

430 Highgate Studios
53–79 Highgate Road
London NW5 1TL
Tel.: 020 7427 3460
Fax: 020 7485 3590
E-mail: info@nfpi.org

An independent charity working to enhance the value and quality of family life. Publications on child-rearing and the family.

National Literacy Trust

www.literacytrust.org.uk

Swire House
59 Buckingham Gate
London SW1E 6AJ
Tel.: 020 7828 2435
Fax: 020 7931 9986
E-mail: contact@literacytrust.org.uk

Information on all aspects of literacy. Publications, book recommendations, advice for parents and schools and much more.

Parent Governor Web Site (DfES)

www.dfes.gov.uk/parep/index.htm

Guidance on the role of a parent governor representative.

Parents Information Network

www.pin.org.uk

Information and advice for parents whose children are using computers and the Internet. Security, protection from viruses and the use of software to filter out unwanted material.

ParentLine Plus

www.parentlineplus.org.uk
430 Highgate Studios
53–79 Highgate Road
London NW5 1TL
Tel.: 0808 800 2222
Text phone: 0800 783 6783

Charity offering support to anyone parenting a child – parents, step-parents, grandparents and foster-parents. Freephone helpline, broad range of publications and courses for parents.

Pre-school Learning Alliance

www.pre-school.org.uk

69 King's Cross Road
London WC1X 9LL
Tel.: 020 7833 0991
Fax: 020 7837 4942
E-mail: pla@pre-school.org.uk

A national educational charity and umbrella body, linking community-based pre-schools. Information and advice on all aspects of work in the pre-school field.

Family 2000 Onwards

www.family2000onwards.com

Information and support site for parents, grandparents and children of divorce. Includes articles on all aspects of family life, and reviews of books for parents.

Department for Education and Skills parents' web site

www.dfes.gov.uk

About your child's education and how you can help. A huge amount of information on every aspect of school and pre-school.

LEA and school addresses

www.dfes.gov.uk/othaddr.htm

This site contains the addresses of UK education departments, local education authorities in England, secondary schools and 16–18 schools and colleges.

USEFUL ADDRESSES

OFSTED (The Office for Standards in Education)
www.ofsted.gov.uk

OFSTED inspection reports can be viewed on this site.

Scottish Executive Parent Zone
www.ngflscotland.gov.uk/parentzone/index.asp

Information for parents on all aspects of education in Scotland.

Department of Education Northern Ireland web site
www.deni.gov.uk

Further Reading

Green, Christopher, *Toddler Taming: The guide to your child from one to four*. Transworld, 1999.

Holt, John, *How Children Learn*. Penguin 1991. *How Children Fail*. Penguin, 1990. *Teach Your Own: A hopeful path for education*. Lighthouse, 1997.
Fascinating insights into the way children learn, from a lifelong teacher and educational consultant.

Lawson, Sarah, *Helping Children Cope with Bullying*. Sheldon Press, 1994.
Provides the practical advice and information parents need to prevent and tackle bullying confidently and effectively.

Pearce, John, *Bad Behaviour*. Thorsons, 1989. *Parents' Guide To Positive Discipline*. Vermillion, 1998.

WH Smith Parents Guide: Homework. WH Smith, 2000.
Covers the important issues of your child's primary education and answers the questions most frequently asked by parents.

Index

accountability 43
after-school activities 1
appeals: school choice 19–20
attendance: absenteeism 97–8;
    home–school agreements
    92; parents' legal
    obligations 90
attention deficit hyperactivity
    disorder (ADHD) 110

bicycles 69
board of governors:
    complaints to 95–6
boredom: curriculum changes
    42–3
bullying 43, 98; children
    keeping quiet 103–4;
    effective actions against
    16–17; expectations of the
    school 103; indications of
    98–101; keeping a diary
    102–3; reporting 102–3;
    school policy on 16–17;
    signs of stress 63–4;
    single-sex schools 11–12;
    by a teacher 104–5

childminders 3
children: basic personal skills
    67; discussing reports with
    26–7; enjoyment of school
    44–5; expectations of 37–9;
    less academic 115;
    motivating 39–41; reasons
    for absenteeism 97;
    teenagers 38;
    underachievers 113–15
Children's Home-Based
    Education Association 121
communication: contacting
    teachers 21–4;
    home–school agreements
    92; how to approach
    complaints 96; listening
    52–3; making concerns
    known to school 93–6;
    parents' associations 33;
    parents' evenings 27–31;
    reports 24–7; school
    governors 33–4; workshops
    32
complaints procedure 94–6
computers: the internet 75–6;
    use at home 75
confidence: home education
    120; parents' role in
    building 47–53; practical
    steps 50–3

day nursery 3
decision-making, children's
    51

depression 65, 101
disability *see* special needs
discipline 43; being consistent 51–2; exclusion 107; hearing about bad behaviour 105–6; pre-schools 5; sanctions and rewards 106–7
dyslexia 110
dyspraxia 110, 130–1

Early Education scheme 2
Education Act (1966) 117
Education Otherwise 121
emotions: depression 65, 101; indications of bullying 98–101; special needs 123
environment 5
equipment 80–1
Examination Appeals Board 107
exams and tests: appeals procedure 107–8; coursework assessment 77; modular approach 44; primary school 78; rewards 50; secondary school 78–80; stress 78–9
exclusion 107
exercise 69

financial difficulties: buying uniforms 70–1

gender: academic achievement 11; bullying 11–12; motivation 45–6

gifted children: common characteristics 109–10; parents' role 111–12; possible problems of 110–11; schools' role 111–12

hand–eye co-ordination 110
head teachers 95
health: depression 65; exercise 61–3; nutrition 57–61; relation to learning 55–6; sleep 56–7; stress 63–4
Health Education Authority 61–2
Helping Children Cope with Bullying (Lawson) 104
home education: help for parents 121; legal obligations 117; qualifications for 118–19; reasons for 117–18; social contact 119–21
home–school agreements 90–3
homework: age guidelines 83; clubs 86; content of 83–4; diaries 86; helping with 84–5; home–school agreements 90; reference books 74; school policy 87; teacher feedback 86–7

independent schools 10–11
Independent Schools Council (ISC) 14

individuality: personal appearance 71–2; pre-schools 5
Internet safety 75–6
IQ scores 111

language skills: difficulties with 110; English as a second language 77; help with 76–7; reading 72–4; special needs 130–1
Lawson, Sarah: *Helping Children Cope with Bullying* 104
league tables *see* performance tables
libraries 74
local education authorities (LEAs): absenteeism 97; complaints to 96; special needs 123, 124, 127–9, 131
love and confidence 48

motivation: and gender 45–6; from parents 39–41; recent educational reforms 42–4

National Association for Gifted Children 109
National Council of Parent–Teacher Associations 33
nursery schools: types of 3–4
nutrition: importance 57–8; meals 59–61; under- and over-weight children 58

Office for Standards in Education (OFSTED) 34; bad schools 43; primary school information 14–15

parent–teacher associations 14, 33
parents: associations 33; building confidence 47–53; expectations 37–9; good enough parenting 53–4; helping at school 31–2; legal obligations of 89–90; own school experiences 41–2; teachers' perceptions of 93–4; workshops for 32
parents' evenings 27–31
performance evaluation: bad schools 43; choosing a school 15–16; tables 15–16
personal appearance: individualism 71–2; uniforms 69–70
play and relaxation 80
playgroups 2
pre-schools: categories of 2–4; choosing 1; grants for 2; reception classes 4; special needs 124; what to look for 4–6
primary schools: contacting the teacher 21–2; gathering information about 12–13; helping in 31–2; looking ahead to secondary 8; oversubscription and appeals 17–20; readiness

for 6–7; reception classes
4; reports 25; special needs
124–5; tests 78; visiting
13–14; when to apply 17

readiness for school 6–7
reading: early preparation 72;
older children 73–4;
primary school 72–3
relationships: building
confidence 48–9
relevance 44
reports 24–5; discussing with
your child 26–7
rewards 50

SATs 24
school governors 33–4
schools: catchment areas 1;
choosing 1; obligations of
90; parents' own memories
of 41–2; recent reforms
42–4
secondary schools: backpacks
and equipment 80–1;
considering primary schools
8; contacting teachers
23–4; exams 78–80; parent
help 32; reports 25; special
needs 125; when to apply
17
Secretary of State for
Education 96
security 48
self-esteem 39
siblings 41
single-sex/co-educational

schools: academic
achievement 11
social life: home education
119–21; out of catchment
area 1
special needs: defining 123–4;
pre-school children 124;
primary and secondary
school 124–5; progress at
school 125–6; SEN
coordinator 126–7;
specialist schools 9, 128–9;
statutory assessment 127–8,
129; tribunal 128 see also
gifted children
specialist schools: types of 9
state schools 8–9; compared
to independents 10–11
stress: exams 79; recognition
and coping 63–4
supervision, quality of 5

teachers: bullying by 104–5;
complaints to 95;
contacting 21–4; form
tutors 23; homework
feedback 86–7; parents'
evenings 28–31; as people
34–5; special needs 126–7
teenagers 38
transport 1, 67–9

underachievers 113–14;
comparison of development
114–15
uniforms 69–71
university 38–9